Kit HACKNEY, ANN $19.75
~~Johnson~~

Epic Adventure - Texas

DATE DUE

2-23-86			
APR 6 '92			

Imperial Public Library
Imperial, Texas

- DEMCO

IMPERIAL PUBLIC LIBRARY
P.O. BOX 307
IMPERIAL, TEXAS 79743

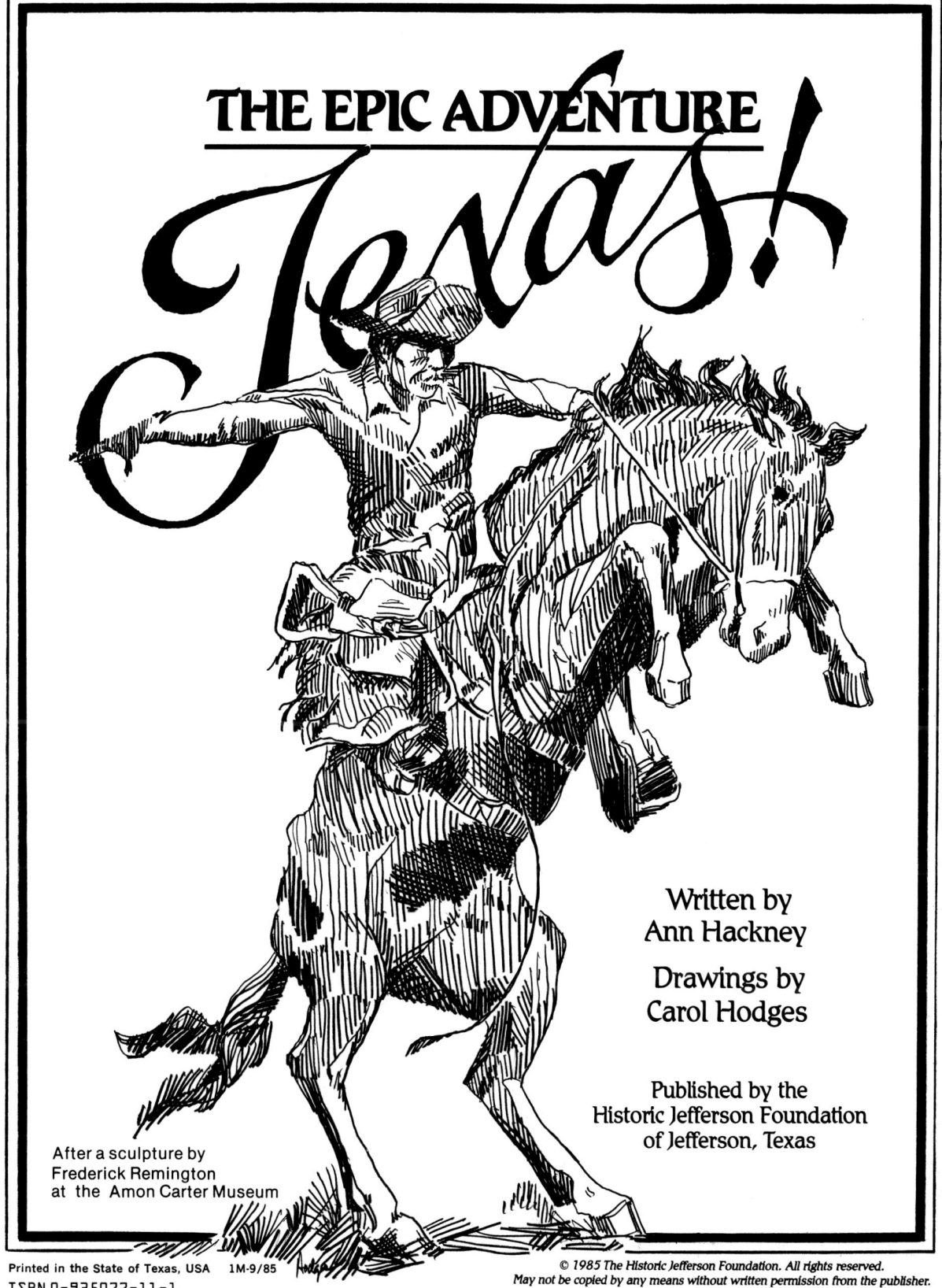

THE EPIC ADVENTURE
Texas!

Written by
Ann Hackney

Drawings by
Carol Hodges

Published by the
Historic Jefferson Foundation
of Jefferson, Texas

After a sculpture by
Frederick Remington
at the Amon Carter Museum

Printed in the State of Texas, USA   1M-9/85
ISBN 0-935077-11-1
Library of Congress Card No. 85-24854

© 1985 The Historic Jefferson Foundation. All rights reserved.
May not be copied by any means without written permission from the publisher.

Lady Bird Johnson shown with native Texas wildflowers: Indian blanket, wild honeysuckle, rock nettle, and bridle wreath.

The Historic Jefferson Foundation is a non-profit, historical society dedicated to education and to the preservation of our Texas heritage.

INTRODUCTION

TEXAS is a legend.

It is the land of cowboys and Indians, the great oil boom and a vital space center. It is the land of wide skies, coastal waters and piney woods—the land of industrious and daring men and women whose vision, resolute will and passionate beliefs have shaped the character of a state.

To know their history and to hear their songs is to share in their dangers, ache with their losses, and soar with their victories. It is to experience TEXAS—their TEXAS—our TEXAS—in all of its boldness and grandeur. It is to share in their honor—share in their glory—and to know that because of these brave men and women, TEXAS lives the legend still.

Lady Bird Johnson

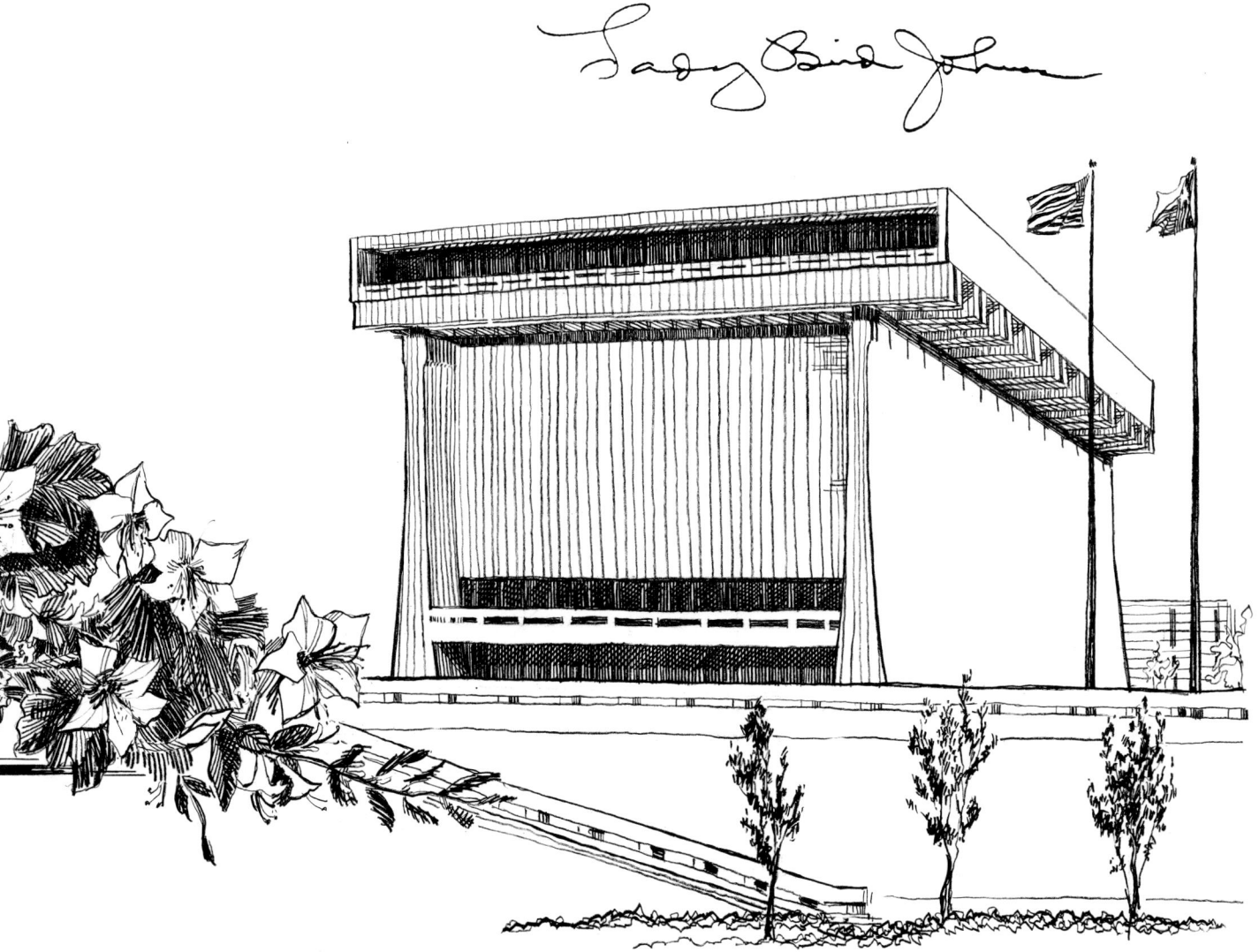

Lyndon Baines Johnson Library, Austin

NATURAL REGIONS

Texas is a land of sudden and dramatic changes! It is a challenging land—and has been from the beginning.

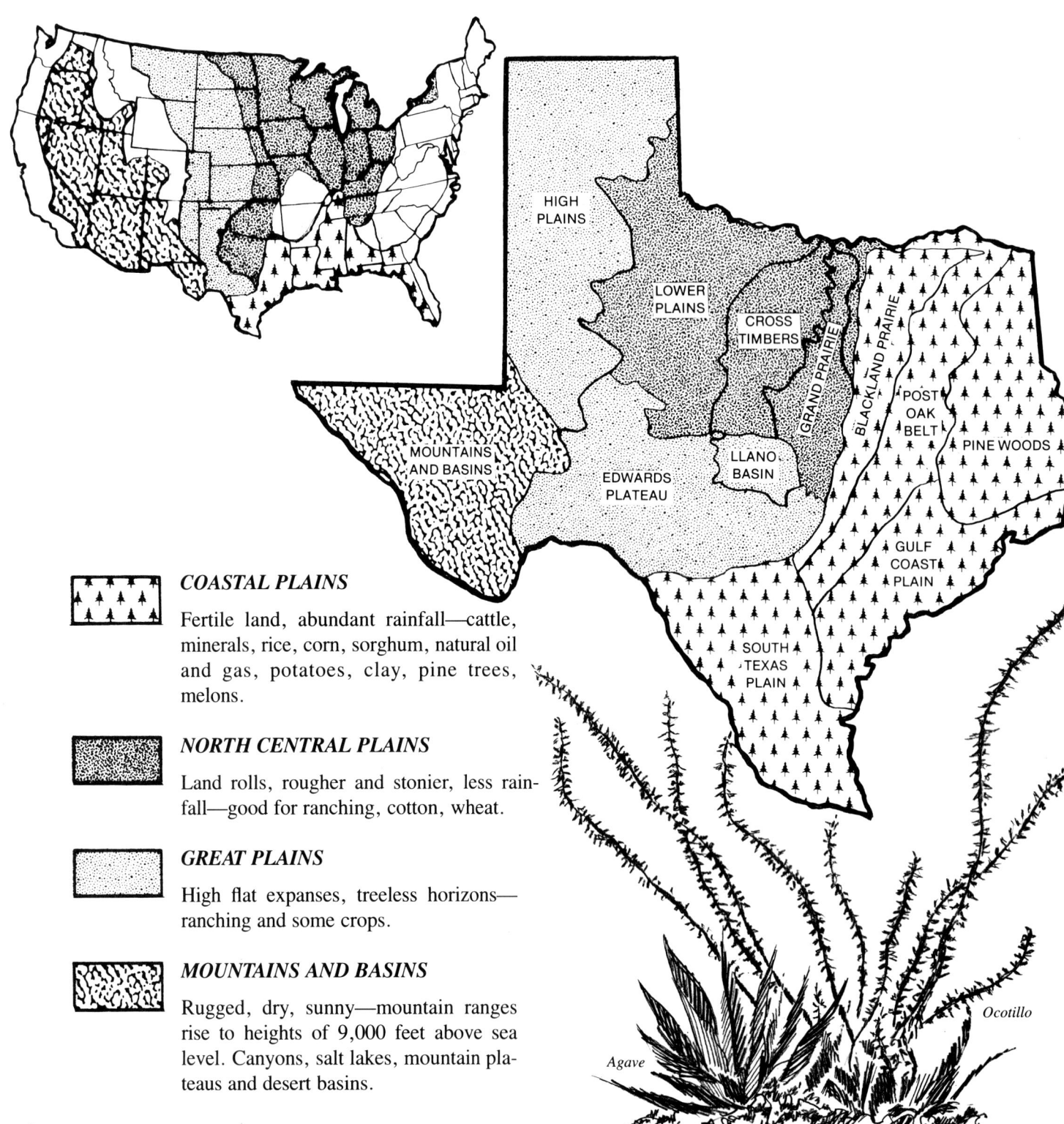

COASTAL PLAINS

Fertile land, abundant rainfall—cattle, minerals, rice, corn, sorghum, natural oil and gas, potatoes, clay, pine trees, melons.

NORTH CENTRAL PLAINS

Land rolls, rougher and stonier, less rainfall—good for ranching, cotton, wheat.

GREAT PLAINS

High flat expanses, treeless horizons—ranching and some crops.

MOUNTAINS AND BASINS

Rugged, dry, sunny—mountain ranges rise to heights of 9,000 feet above sea level. Canyons, salt lakes, mountain plateaus and desert basins.

TEXAS! . . . the very name is exciting! We think of wildcatting and broncobusting . . . of tall tales and brave deeds . . . of heroic men and women who were hard riding and hard living, and whose souls were at one with the land.

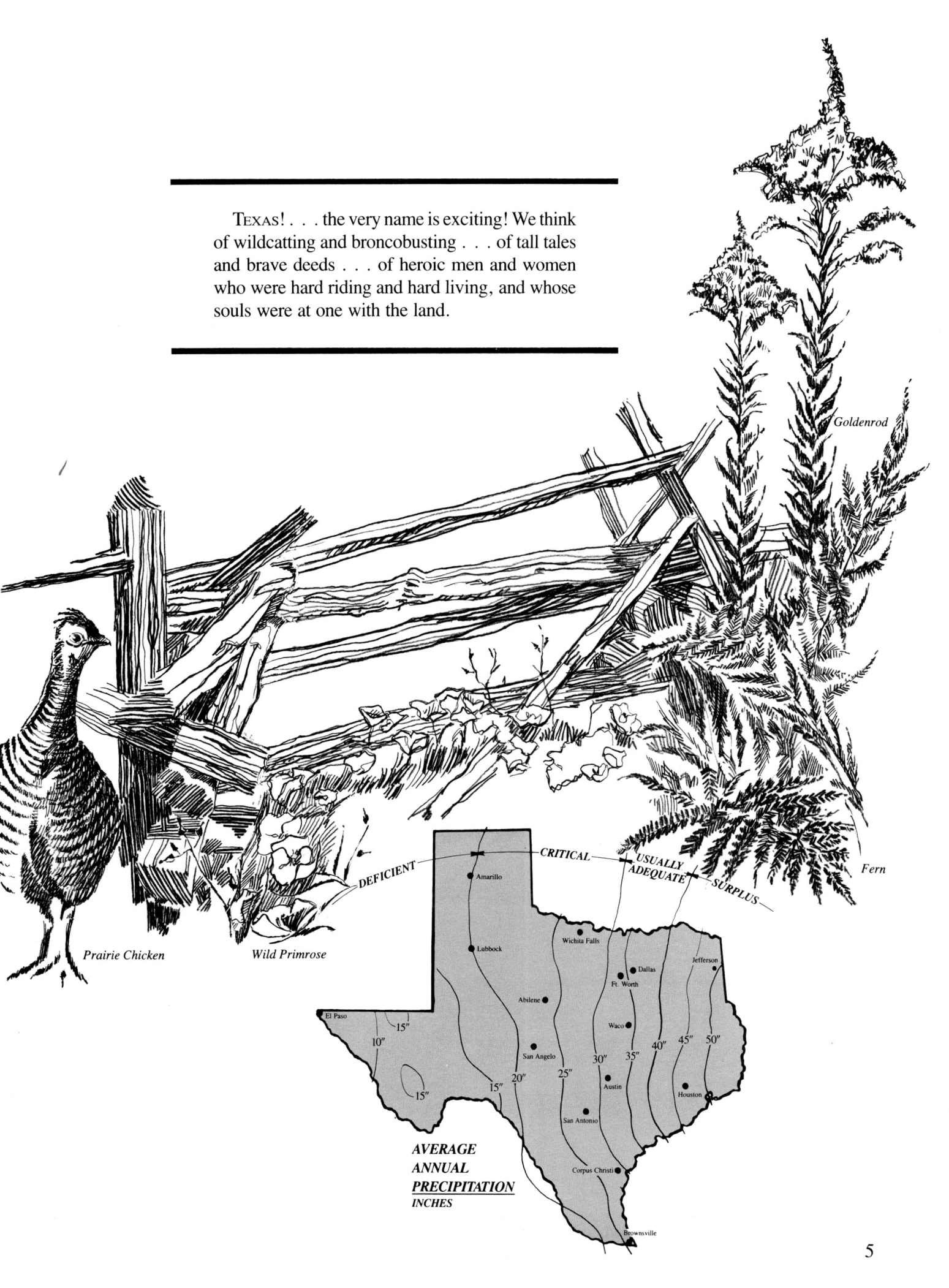

PREHISTORIC TEXAS

PALEO-AMERICAN STAGE: 15,000 to 5000 B.C.

Early man first entered the land we now call Texas during the Ice Age. Nomadic tribes had followed the herds of animals that crossed the Bering Strait in search of food.

The first arrivals required extraordinary bravery to hunt the great mammoth, mastodon, bison, and giant ground sloth that prowled the plains. They killed these huge animals with flint-tipped throwing sticks—sometimes surrounding them at waterholes—or they would stampede the herds off cliffs.

The meat they roasted in great limestone cooking areas; then they sat around the fires drying the skins for clothing and flaking new flint and bone tools.

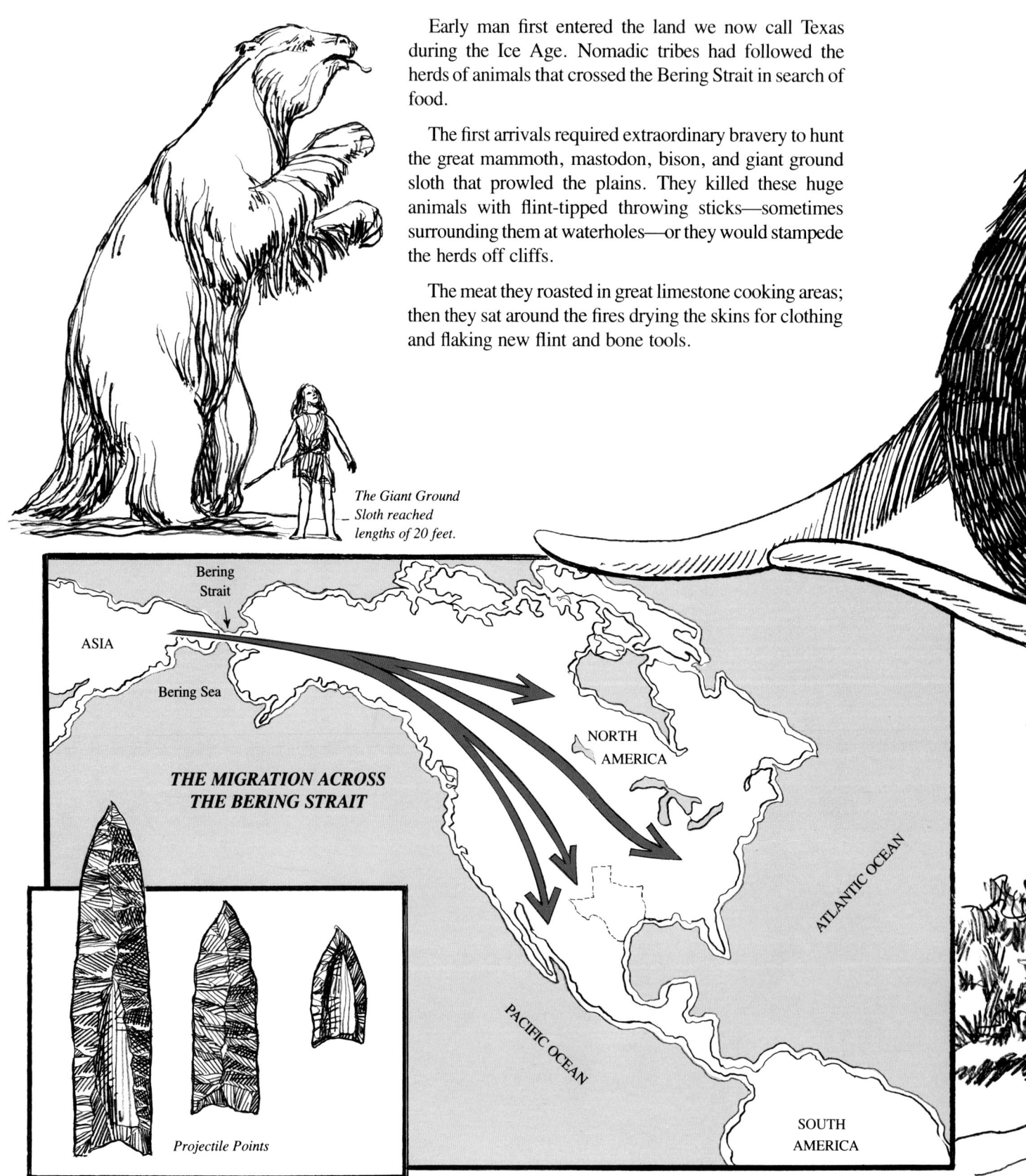

The Giant Ground Sloth reached lengths of 20 feet.

THE MIGRATION ACROSS THE BERING STRAIT

Projectile Points

Woolly Mammoths grew to 13 feet with tusks of over 9 feet.

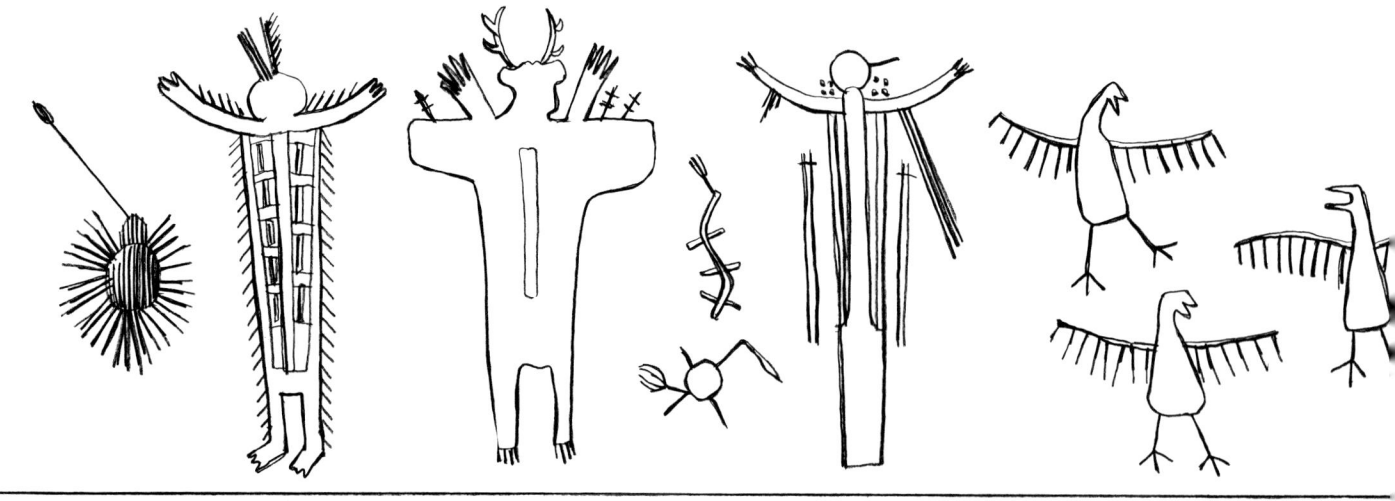

ROCK ART

ARCHAIC STAGE: 8000 B.C. to A.D. 1500

Before the land bridge at the Bering Strait disappeared into the sea, other men had crossed from Asia. They were Mongoloid in ancestry—hunters and gatherers. For thousands of years they continued to come into Texas. They called themselves "The People" or "The Real People." Later, Europeans would call them "Indians."

These hunting tribes published stories of their hopes and struggles on the walls of rock-shelters or smooth bluffs. Their pictographs show an enjoyment of rituals—of dressing up in costumes. They were people of no small imagination who sought higher meaning to their lives.

With the invention of the bow, life became easier; but it was still harsh.

The Big Bend region.

INDIANS

NEO-AMERICAN STAGE: 3000 B.C. to A.D. 1500

Later, Indian tribes developed different customs and different languages. The land had a great deal to do with the way they lived.

WESTERN GULF ▶
CULTURE

The tribes living near the Gulf could obtain food from the sea. They also had an ample supply of wild plants, spiders, worms, and lizards to eat. Food was plentiful.

SOUTHEASTERN ▶
CULTURE

The tribes in the piney woods of East Texas hunted game and fished in the streams. They became some of our first farmers. Cultivated crops made their lives more secure. They did not need to depend upon seasonal wild foods. This meant they could put up permanent homes and develop villages.

PLAINS CULTURE ▶

The tribes living on the plains found that the buffalo supplied their needs, and they migrated with the herds.

PUEBLOAN CULTURE ▶

The tribes living to the far west needed water, so they devised an irrigation system to nurture their gardens.

The Indians' contribution to civilization—to all of us who came after them—was enormous: three-fifths of all of the world's agricultural wealth today comes from plants first farmed by Indians of the Americas.

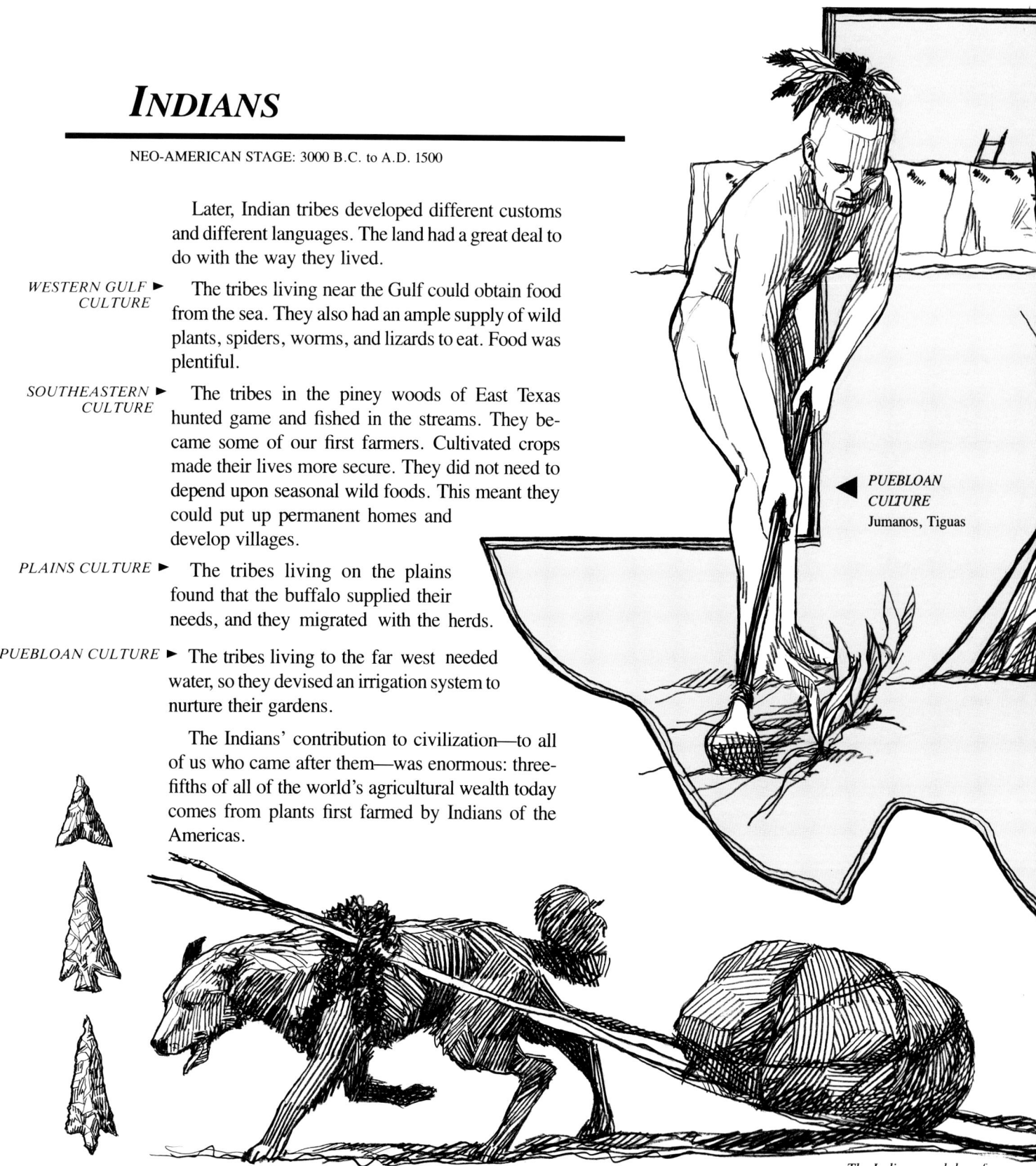

◀ PUEBLOAN
CULTURE
Jumanos, Tiguas

The Indians used dogs for many purposes.

PLANTS CULTIVATED BY THE INDIANS OF THE AMERICAS:

Corn, Irish potatoes, sweet potatoes, several varieties of beans, squash, pumpkins, peanuts, chocolate, rubber, cotton, and tobacco are a few of the plants first farmed by Indians of the Americas.

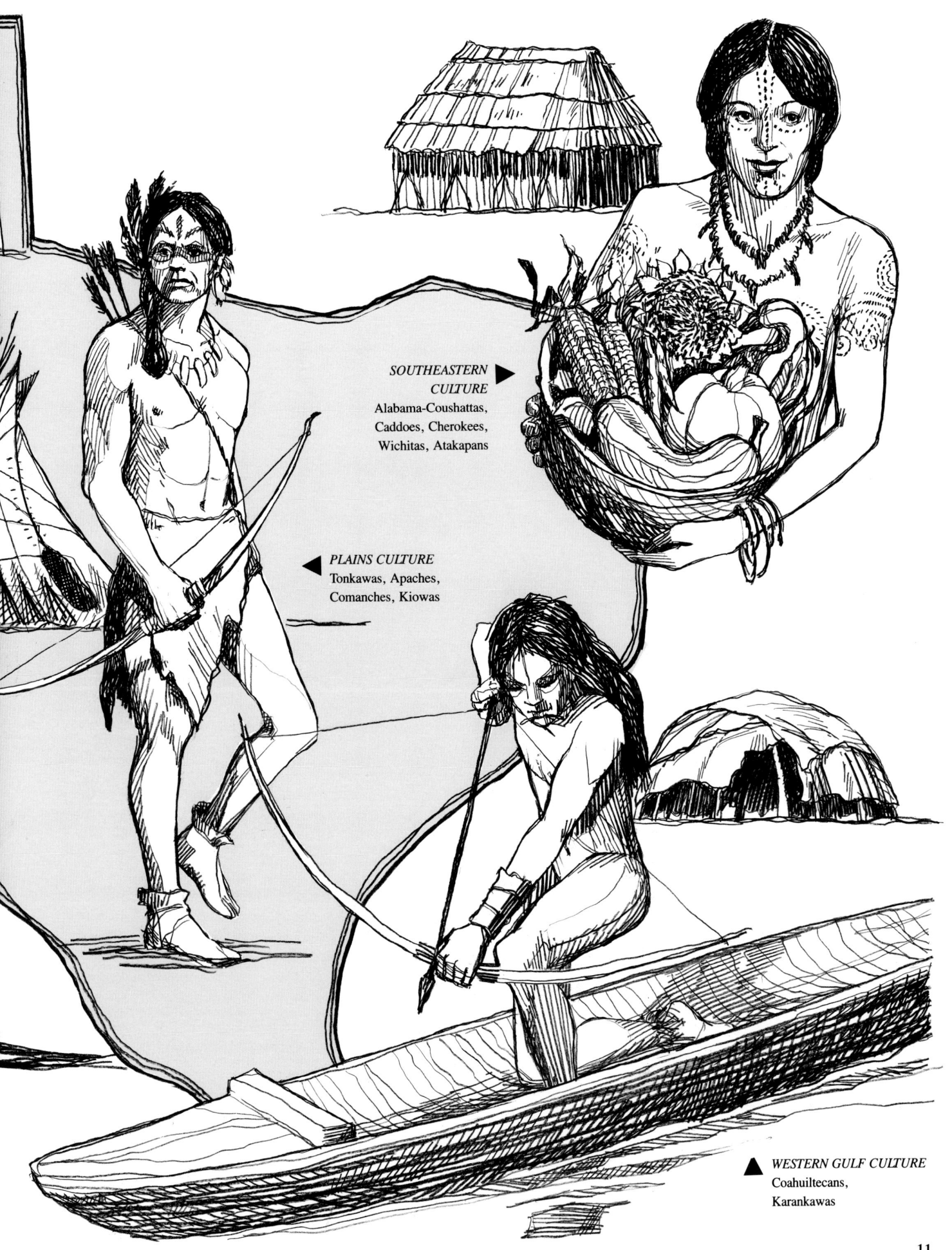

SOUTHEASTERN CULTURE
Alabama-Coushattas, Caddoes, Cherokees, Wichitas, Atakapans

PLAINS CULTURE
Tonkawas, Apaches, Comanches, Kiowas

WESTERN GULF CULTURE
Coahuiltecans, Karankawas

TEJAS . . . TEXAS

When the Spanish asked an Indian the name of his tribe, he answered: *"Tayshas"* . . . meaning "friend." The Spanish pronounced the word: *"Tejas"* . . . or *TEXAS*.

"Ay, Ay, Ay, Ay, Canta y no llores
Porque cantando se alegran,
Cielito Lindo los corazones"
    Excerpt from *CIELITO LINDO*,
    an old Spanish Folk Song

THE SPANISH

HISTORIC STAGE: A.D. 1500 to the present

In the blistering summer of 1540, a powerful invader suddenly burst upon the wilds of Texas. Holding high the red and gold banner of Spain and brandishing the cross and the sword, the Spanish came to seek gold and to convert the heathen to God.

Coronado and his army must have seemed awesome to the Indians. They wore shining steel armor and rode fantastic creatures called "horses." At first the Indians thought that the horse with its rider was a single terrifying beast. The Spanish had guns and gun powder, too . . . and other fantastic creatures called cattle, sheep, goats, donkeys, hogs, and chickens.

These conquerors were bold men—disciplined men—men fired by religious zeal. They brought with them writing and the recording of history. They brought money and the wheel and concepts of law and architecture . . . and they named the rivers and mountains.

Two-thirds of the recorded history of Texas is Spanish history.

Palo Duro Canyon

THE FRENCH

In 1684, Robert Cavelier La Salle and a group of soldiers and settlers missed the mouth of the Mississippi River and landed instead on the coast of Texas. La Salle had already claimed Louisiana and named it for the French king, but now this expedition was doomed to failure. Two ships sank; and the third sailed back to France, stranding the landing party. La Salle himself was killed by his own men; and the settlers either died of disease, or were killed or captured by Indians.

Yet France had planted its flag on Texas soil; and Spain, hearing of the intruders, feverishly sought to settle the new land before its new competitors could take hold.

The French in time became traders with the Indians, peaceably accepting their customs, and often living among them.

Au clair de la lune
Mon ami Pierrot,
Prête-moi ta plume
Pour écrire un mot;
Excerpt from *AU CLAIR DE LA LUNE*

SPANISH MISSIONS

As Spain moved quickly to colonize Texas through mission settlements, priests, accompanied by soldiers, were sent to convert the Indians, teach them skills, and to keep the new land in the grip of Spanish control.

Life in the missions was very different from the life the Indians had known. There was a set schedule. Each day began with religious studies. After breakfast the men were taught blacksmithing, carpentry, farming, and the care of farm animals. The women molded pottery or learned to weave. The evenings were devoted to more religious studies.

This life proved too rigid for the Indians who had lived close to nature. They could not tolerate it. They sickened from the diseases brought over from Europe. The war-like tribes raided the missions and made life generally miserable for the inhabitants.

Mission after mission failed as the Indians died or disappeared back into the wilderness.

Libera me, Domine,
  de morte aeterna
In die illa tremenda:
Quando caeli movendi sunt et terra:
Dum veneris judicare saeculum per ignem.
  An ancient Catholic Response in Gregorian chant.

Mission San José y San Miguel de Aguayo, San Antonio

Indians on Horseback

Between 1600 and 1650, a great revolution occurred on the Texas plains . . . Indians on horseback. Coronado had brought the Spanish mustang into Texas. Some of the creatures were lost, some stolen, but the horses multiplied.

The mustang was fast, desert bred, and could live from water hole to water hole. Before the horse, the Indians had been no match for the mounted, armored invaders—but now they could match them in speed and mobility; and soon the Indians were striking at the mission settlements and melting away into the endless plains.

The first time mounted Indians topped a ridge, they changed the tide of history. Unlike the Aztec tribes, the Texas Indians of the plains were able to prevail for three hundred years.

*While taking refreshments
we heard a low yell,
The whoop of Sioux Indians
coming up from the dell;
We sprang to our rifles
with a flash in each eye.
"Boys," says our brave leader,
"we'll fight till we die."*
Excerpt from *SIOUX INDIANS*

ANGLO-AMERICAN SETTLERS

The first Anglo-American frontiersmen who crossed the mountains and the Mississippi River to come to Texas turned their backs upon the softer life on the eastern coast. They were hunters and trappers determined to master the Texas wilds. Not only could they use a tomahawk as well as the Indian, they were equipped with the long-barreled Kentucky rifle. They would hunt the game, then sell the hides and move on.

Soon to come were the equally tough hunter/farmers and their families. These too were skilled in tracking game, but they also cleared small plots of land and put in crops. They built crude cabins with dirt floors. Their children had to be tough too. They grew up fast, worked hard, faced hunger, and the constant threat of attack by Indians and outlaws; but the settlers endured.

Rise you up, my partner dear,
And present to me your hand,
'Cause I know you want to marry,
And I'd like to be the man.
And I'll take you out to Texas,
Where I know you want to go,
And we'll rally round the canebrake,
And shoot the buffalo.
Excerpt from SHOOT THE BUFFALO

The Big Thicket.

FILIBUSTERS* AND PIRATES

The frontier also attracted adventurers—fast-riding, hard-living, daring men—who several times tried to seize control of Texas and create a new republic; but Spanish troops defeated them each time.

Spain by now was a nation in decline, her soldiers no longer able to stop the Indian raids in Texas. The Spanish Crown was very distant from this wild, new land, and was beginning to tire of the troubles visited upon it by traders, smugglers, pirates, and revolutionaries.

One of the most successful buccaneers was the legendary pirate, Jean Lafitte. He actually created his own republic on Galveston Island and lived there in princely, roguish splendor in his red-painted home with cannons mounted in the upper windows.

*Filibuster: An American, who took part in developing discords and rebellions.

Oh, my name is Captain Kidd, as I sailed, as I sailed,
My name is Captain Kidd, as I sailed;
My name is Captain Kidd, God's laws I did forbid,
And most wickedly I did, as I sailed, as I sailed.
   Excerpt from **CAPTAIN KIDD**

THE OLD THREE HUNDRED

Although Spain ruled Texas for almost three hundred years, very few Spanish citizens were willing to move there. So in 1820, thinking American settlers loyal to Spain might stand between the Indians and the mission churches, the Spanish government made a deal with Moses Austin. He was offered large tracts of land for three hundred families. Moses Austin died; but his son, Stephen F. Austin, settled two hundred and ninety-seven American families under Mexican rule.

Most of these families brought slaves with them. This created a self-styled gentry or planter class, causing strained feelings among the small farmers who worked their own land.

This planter class was soon shaping the customs and manners of Texas and exporting cotton, tallow, pork, beef, lard, mules, and other commodities. The influence of Spain grew weaker all the time.

Come all you young ladies and listen to my noise,
And don't you go marrying those Texas boys,
'Cause if you do your life's gonna be
Johnnycake and venison and sassafras tea,
Johnnycake and venison and sassafras tea.
    Excerpt from TEXAS BOYS

MEXICAN RULE

After Mexico had won her independence from Spain, Texas came under Mexican rule. In the next fifteen years, thousands of Americans were allowed to settle the land under promoters and *empresarios* like Austin. Thousands more illegally crossed the borders from the United States.

Soon the Americans outnumbered the Mexican settlers. The Mexican government was alarmed. What happened if the settlers decided to become a separate people, wanting their own nation?

To head off the Americans, Mexico closed the borders, sent in troops, set up tax offices, and began to remove arms the settlers used to protect themselves against Indian raids.

The Mexican government seriously misjudged these settlers. They prized their freedom. As Austin wrote of his people: they "felt that they were sovereigns; for they were beyond the arm of government or of the law, unless it pleased them to be controlled." And it did not please them. Serious trouble began.

Allá en el rancho grande,
allá donde vivía,
habia una rancherita,
que alegre me decía,
que alegre me decía.
Excerpt from *EL RANCHO GRANDE*

General Antonio López de Santa Anna,
President and dictator of the
Republic of Mexico.

Texas Volunteers

When the word went out that Texans might take a stand against Mexico, volunteers rushed to cross the border from the United States to assist them. They came because they had relatives in Texas, or because they thought Texas was meant to be part of the United States, or because they were promised land . . . or simply because they liked a good scrap!

With the cry "To arms!! To arms!! Now is the day and now is the hour!", the men marched off to fight for Texas.

*O that gal, that pretty little gal,
The gal I left behind me.
I'm going to stop and stay all night
With the gal I left behind me.*
    Excerpt from THE GAL I LEFT BEHIND ME

FLAGS OF THE VOLUNTEERS

Top row, left to right:
  The Alabama Volunteers
  Goliad Declaration of Independence
  The Georgia Volunteers
  The Naval Flag of the Revolution

Bottom row, left to right:
  The Louisiana Volunteers
  The Texas Volunteer Army of the People
  The Harrisburg Volunteers
  The Kentucky Volunteers
  The Lynchburg Volunteers
  The San Felipe Company

THE REVOLUTION

When war began, Anglo-American, Black-American, Mexican, Irish, Polish, Italian, Jewish, and German Texans rose up to fight for independence.

While one group of Texans was hurriedly writing the Texas Declaration of Independence at Washington-on-the-Brazos, members of another group were paying with their lives for the time to organize. From the walls of the Alamo these men could see Santa Anna's red flag and hear the Mexican bugler blaring the death-song, "Degüello"—no prisoners would be taken. For thirteen days, one hundred and eighty-three men fought thousands of Mexican troops; but on March 6, 1836, with an all-out assault by Santa Anna's army, the battle of the Alamo was over. It cost the lives of the best known heroes in Texas history.

When the Alamo fell, Texas families panicked and left their homes and lands in a wild rush for safety. Santa Anna marched across Texas, determined to crush the rebellion.

In Goliad, Fannin and his men were forced to surrender to the Mexican General Urrea. Fannin and three hundred and fifty men were executed on Palm Sunday, March 27, 1836.

As the news of the Goliad massacre spread across Texas, even more families gathered their belongings and took to the roads in flight; but Sam Houston retreated just long enough to gather his men—then they turned and marched to meet Santa Anna at San Jacinto River and the Buffalo Bayou.

On April 21, 1836, the Texas troops marched boldly across an open prairie to within forty yards of the enemy lines, and then they opened fire. The drums beat, the fifes played "Come to the Bower" . . . and with the blood of their loved ones and friends still fresh in their memories, the Texans charged! "REMEMBER THE ALAMO!" they cried, "REMEMBER THE ALAMO!" Within eighteen minutes the battle was won. It has been called one of the most decisive battles in history. Texas had won her freedom.

Mission San Antonio de Valero—the Alamo

To the people of Texas and all Americans in the world—

Fellow Citizens and Compatriots—
 I am besieged by a thousand or more of the Mexicans under Santa Anna—I have sustained a continual Bombardment & cannonade for 24 hours & have not lost a man—the enemy has demanded a surrender at discretion, otherwise the garrison are to be put to the sword if the Fort is taken—I have answered the demand with a cannon shot, & our flag still waves proudly from the walls—I shall never surrender or retreat. Then, I call on you in the name of Liberty, of patriotism & everything dear to the American character to come to our aid with all dispatch—The enemy is receiving reinforcements daily & will no doubt increase to three or four thousand in four or five days. If this call is neglected, I am **determined** to sustain myself as long as possible & die like a soldier who never forgets what is due to his own honor & that of his country—

Victory Or Death
William Barret Travis
Lt. Col. comdt.

P.S. **The Lord** is on our side. When the enemy appeared in sight we had not three bushels of corn—we have since found in deserted houses 80 or 90 bushels & got into the walls 20 or 30 head of Beeves—

Travis

Will you come to the bower
 I have shaded for you?
I have decked it with roses
 all spangled with dew.
Will you, will you, will you, will you,
 Come to my bower?
Will you, will you, will you, will you,
 Come to my bower?
 Excerpt from *COME TO THE BOWER*

San Jacinto Monument

THE REPUBLIC OF TEXAS

"Victory or Death"
WILLIAM BARRET TRAVIS

"Colonel Neil and myself have come to the solemn resolution that we had rather die in these ditches than give it up to the enemy."
JAMES BOWIE

"I leave this rule for others when I am dead, be always sure you are right, then go ahead."
DAVID CROCKETT

"The prosperity of Texas has been the object of my labors—the idol of my existence—it has assumed the character of a religion—for the guidance of my thoughts and actions."
STEPHEN F. AUSTIN

"The cultivated mind is the guardian genius of Democracy, and while guided and controlled by virtue, the noblest attribute of man. It is the only dictator that free men acknowledge, and the only security which free men desire."
MIRABEAU B. LAMAR

"If Texas demands your service or your life, in her cause, stand by her."
SAM HOUSTON

The Lone Star flag flew proudly over the Republic of Texas for ten years. Under three presidents—Sam Houston, Mirabeau B. Lamar, and Anson Jones—she was guided through Mexican invasions, Indian raids, and growing debts.

Between 1836 at the battle of San Jacinto, and 1846 when Texas became a state, the population tripled. The people established public schools, a state library, and made provision for universities. Texas' own navy sailed the high seas. The government opened diplomatic relations with England and France; and, daringly, claimed the territory from the Rio Grande all the way to the Pacific Ocean.

When Santa Anna's star went down,
The Lone Star rose on high,
And blazed aloft a brilliant light
In freedom's cloudless sky.
Excerpt from TEXAS HEROES

TEXAS RANGERS

The Texas Ranger became one of the most popular legends of the western frontier. This tight-lipped group of mounted men rode to protect the settlers from Mexican attacks from the south and Indian raids from the north and west.

The Rangers wore no uniforms, were not required to salute their officers, and were never drilled. They were said to be quiet-spoken men who, when trouble came, could act with swift and often brutal force. They became so feared the word spread that but one ranger was needed to stop a riot. This world-wide reputation was worth as much to them as the Colt six-shooters they carried.

Armed with a knife, rifle, rope, and two six-guns, the Ranger was able to challenge the plains Indian in his own style of warfare. After an early battle, when the Colt six-shooter was first used, a Commanche war chief said of Jack Hays, the Ranger leader: "I will never again fight Jack Hays, who has a shot for every finger on the hand."

Come all you Texas Rangers
Where ever you may be,
I will tell you of some trouble
That happened unto me . . .
Excerpt from *TEXAS RANGERS*

ETHNIC COSTUMES
left to right:
Chinese, Afro-American,
Lebanese, Polish,
Mexican,
German

Stake-and-rider worm fence

STATEHOOD

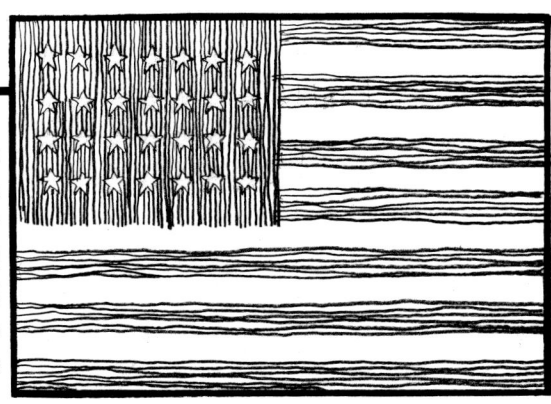

Texas entered the Union as the only state ever to have been a separate nation. She already had her own national history, her own revolutionary war, and national heroes. She had her own flag, navy, and foreign recognition. She brought into the Union one fourth of the land in the entire United States.

Texas also maintained control over her own public lands and was given the unusual right of dividing herself into five separate states, if she chose. There was no state like Texas, and Texans let no one forget it.

In addition to the great wealth of natural resources, Texas is rich in the cultures of many nationalities. Two songs from her diverse ethnic heritage are "Motherless Chile" from the Black culture, and "Muss I Denn" from the German.

Sometimes I feel like a motherless chile,
Sometimes I feel like a motherless chile,
Sometimes I feel like a motherless chile,
Far, far away from home,
A long, long ways from home.
Excerpt from SOMETIMES I FEEL
LIKE A MOTHERLESS CHILE

Muss i denn, muss i denn
Zum Städtele hinaus, Städtele hinaus,
Und du, mei Schatz, bleibst hier?
Excerpt from MUSS I DENN

German rock fence

Mexican picket,
or palisado,
corral fence.

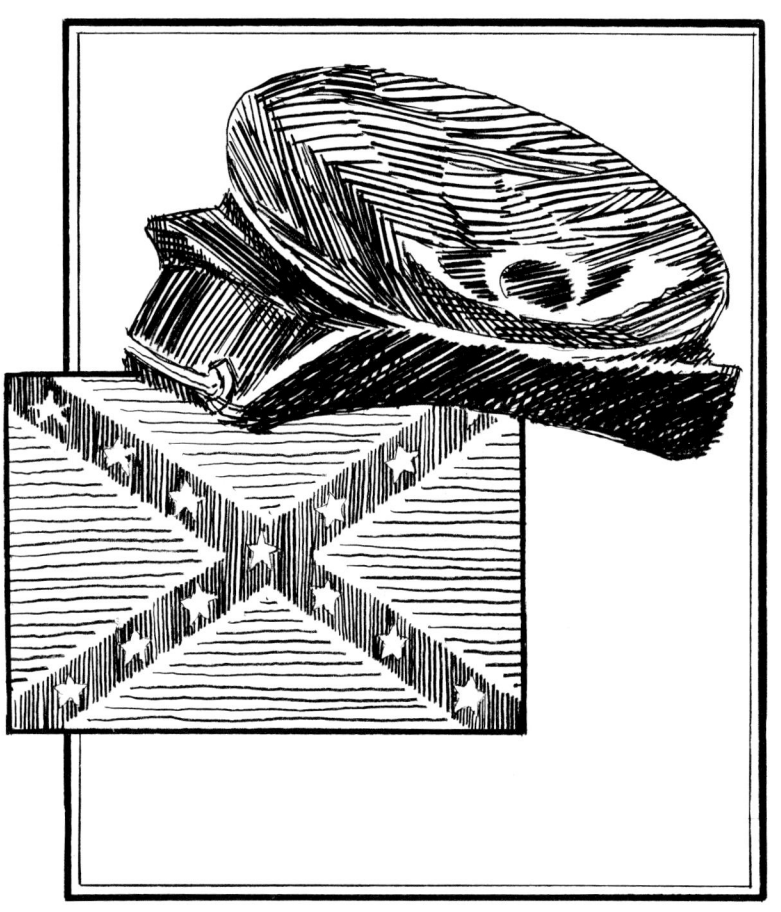

THE CIVIL WAR

During the first fifteen years that Texas was a state, the industrial North of America and the agricultural South were finding it impossible to reconcile their differences over the issues of slavery and states' rights. In 1861, ten southern states left the Union to form the Confederate States of America. Texas joined them—but the governor of Texas, Sam Houston, the hero of San Jacinto, refused to quit the Union and was forced to leave his office.

In the Civil War that followed, about sixty thousand Texans served in the army of the Confederacy, and over two thousand served in the Union army. The state sent vast economic aid to the other southern states, and the last battle of the entire war was fought on Texas soil a month after the Confederacy had already surrendered. For a long time to come many Texans refused to admit the war had been lost.

There's a Yellow Rose in Texas,
that I am going to see,
No other soldier knows her,
no one but only me;
She cried so when I left her,
it like to broke my heart,
And if I ever find her,
we nevermore will part.
Excerpt from THE YELLOW ROSE OF TEXAS

Children's rally for the Confederacy.

RECONSTRUCTION

The war was over, but the wounds took a long time healing. Many of the slaves who had been freed left the land they had worked and wandered from place to place trying to begin a new life. The federal government established the Freedmen's Bureau to help them—but they were exploited nonetheless by unrepentant rebels and unscrupulous foreigners "come down to run things".

The North had been well equipped to win the war, but found it hard to establish the peace. Military rule was set up, and prison stockades were crowded with Texas citizens. Some of those who would not cooperate with the military rule had their homes burned. Hard feelings grew between Texans and Northerners who had been appointed to government offices. These were called "carpetbaggers".

Many Texans remained defiant . . . and sang their defiance in some very tough songs.

Northerners coming into the Reconstruction South were called "carpetbaggers" because often their luggage was made from carpet material.

*I followed old Marse Robert
Three year or nigh about,
Got wounded in three places
And starved at P'int Lookout.
I cotch the rheumatism
A-camping in the snow,
But I killed a mess of Yankees
And I'd like to kill some more.*
Excerpt from
THE UNRECONSTRUCTED REBEL

Steamboats docked in Jefferson during the Reconstruction.

TRAILS WEST

Other Texans put the war and Reconstruction behind them and headed west to that part of Texas that was free and untamed, but nothing had prepared these settlers for the frontier they found there.

The land was harsh and afflicted by drought. The high winds that blew across those open spaces carried off the top soil in great storms of dust. The crops that did not burn in the withering sun were often eaten by swarms of grasshoppers or destroyed by prairie fires. Many settlers actually starved; but others, with grit and wit, dug in their heels and held on to their claims.

Hurrah, for Greer County! The land of the free,
The land of the grasshopper, bedbug, and flea,
I'll sing of its praises and tell of its fame
And starve plumb to death on my government claim.
Excerpt from THE GREER COUNTY BACHELOR

THE SOD HOUSE

Since there was no timber for the construction of houses, the settlers dug about four feet into the ground; then they extended the walls above the ground with large blocks of grassy soil. The house was planked on the inside with wood that they had hauled with them. Sod houses were dark and damp, leaked when it rained, and were full of bugs; but they provided enough shelter for the settlers to hold down their claims.

THE BUFFALO HUNTERS

The farmers and ranchers who opened the western frontier found countless thousands of buffalo grazing on these plains. The grasslands were protected by the Comanche and Kiowa Indians who depended upon the buffalo for their food, clothing, and shelter. These tribes migrated with the herds and saw their way of life threatened as the newcomers began a great slaughter of the buffalo in the early 1870's.

The just completed transcontinental railroad made it possible to ship the hides to eastern markets; but the main purpose for the slaughter was the removal of the Indians' livelihood, forcing them to retreat to the Oklahoma reservations, and clearing the land for crops and cattle. Between 1870 and 1880, thirteen million buffalo were massacred.

The hunters came heavily armed for the three months' stay on the range. They had to be hardy enough to live with danger, filth, the smell of rotting buffalo flesh, the buzzards that circled in waiting, and the back-breaking work.

Our hearts were cased with buffalo hocks,
our souls were cased with steel,
And the hardships of that summer
would nearly make us reel.
Excerpt from THE BUFFALO HUNTERS

THE COWBOY AND THE CATTLE KINGDOM

Once the buffalo were gone, the ancient hunting grounds of the Indians greeted another western hero—the Texas cowboy.

The northern cities boomed after the Civil War; and range cattle which brought about four dollars in Texas, sold for thirty to fifty dollars in the meat markets of Chicago. Trail drives were organized to get Texas cattle to those markets. Between 1866 and 1900, ten million head of cattle left Texas by northern trails.

The drives began with the "rise" of the grass in the spring and continued through the summer. Usually it would take about twelve men to guide a herd of three thousand cattle to market.

The life of the cowboy was for the young and the hardy. There were rainstorms, flash floods, cattle rustlers, stampedes, rattlesnakes, wolves . . . all endured for a monthly wage of some fifteen dollars.

Eventually the railroads made the long trail drives unnecessary, and barbed wire fenced the open plains; but the cowboy lived on—in fact and legend.

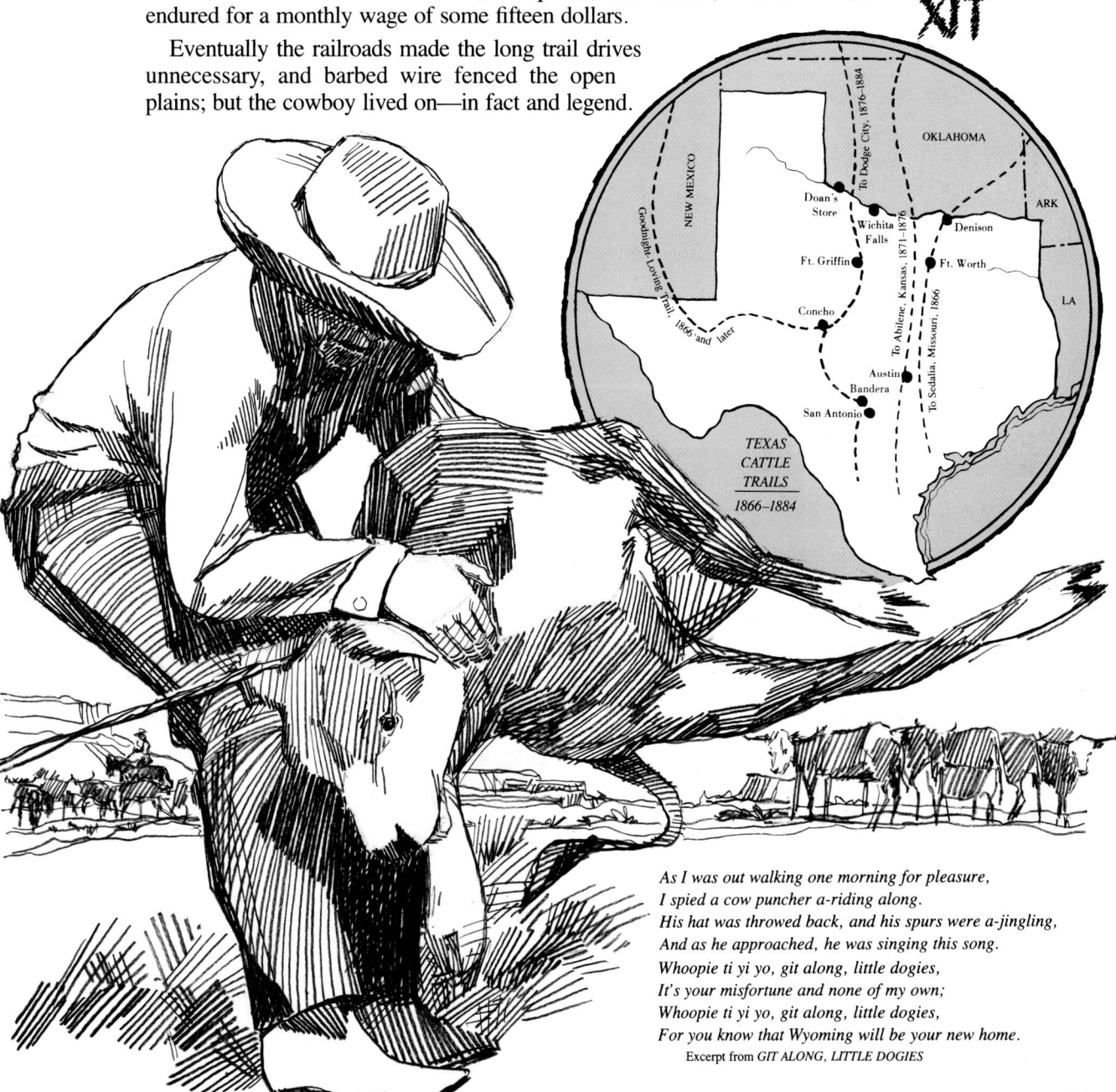

As I was out walking one morning for pleasure,
I spied a cow puncher a-riding along.
His hat was throwed back, and his spurs were a-jingling,
And as he approached, he was singing this song.
Whoopie ti yi yo, git along, little dogies,
It's your misfortune and none of my own;
Whoopie ti yi yo, git along, little dogies,
For you know that Wyoming will be your new home.
  Excerpt from *GIT ALONG, LITTLE DOGIES*

RAILROADS

Texans took to the iron horse as they had taken to the wild mustang. With the east and west coasts only seven days apart, Texans rushed to lay tracks. They saw the railroads as the cheapest and best means of getting their products to larger markets.

To encourage the railroads to invest in Texas, the government gave these companies an area as large as the state of Alabama in public lands. By 1904 Texas led the nation in miles of track and was moving toward industrialization. Lumber, iron ore, salt, cottonseed oil, corn, plows, soap, and many other products soon were reaching eastern markets.

Texas was beginning to pick up speed . . . just like the "Wabash Cannonball".

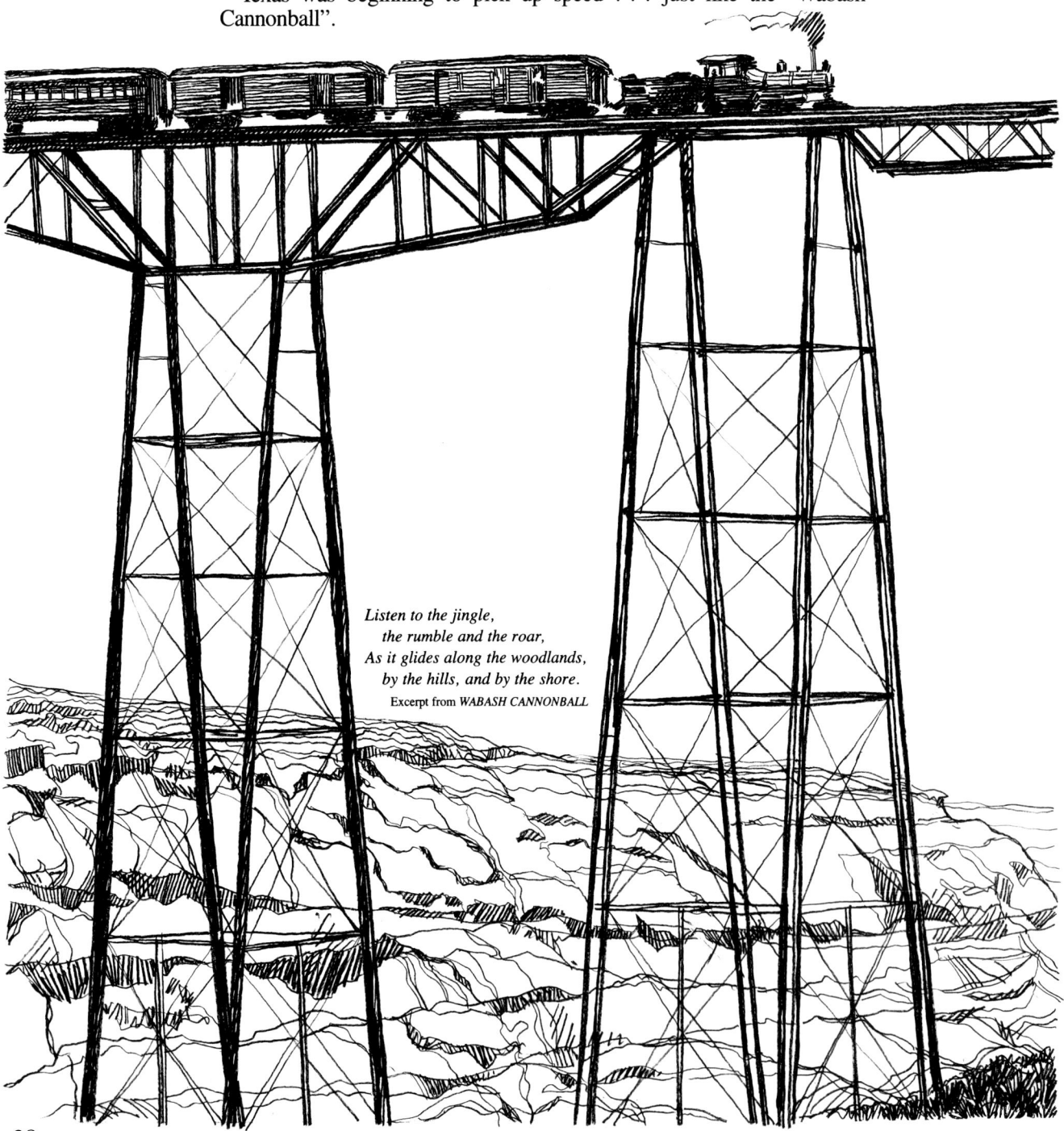

Listen to the jingle,
the rumble and the roar,
As it glides along the woodlands,
by the hills, and by the shore.
Excerpt from WABASH CANNONBALL

RURAL TEXAS

As Texas moved toward the 20th Century, most of the Texans still lived pioneer lives. Eight out of ten Texans lived on farms or in small towns.

In the rural areas, children attended school in one-room schoolhouses. Social activities usually centered around church meetings, quilting bees, or political rallies. Many families still supplied most of their own food and clothing. They had chickens, a cow, their own water well, and a garden.

Holidays were important and festive occasions. On the Fourth of July whole communities would gather for picnics. Many towns had their own singing societies and small bands; and everyone came to town when the circus did.

In a little rosewood casket
That is resting on my stand
Is a package of love letters
Written by my true love's hand.
Excerpt from ROSEWOOD CASKET

Abilene, 1895.

URBAN TEXAS

At the turn of the century, only nineteen years had passed since the last settlers had been killed in Indian raids; yet the cities in Texas were beginning to catch up with the rest of the United States.

Stately homes and impressive business establishments were built. Telephone service linked most of the larger communities, and electricity was available to homes and businesses.

Texans bought cars, and the state built roads. Houston bricked twenty-six miles of streets, and San Antonio paved roads with mesquite wood. Eventually an eighteen mile an hour speed limit had to be imposed on these new contraptions to insure public safety.

By 1901, the gusher Spindletop spewed oil one hundred feet into the air; and by 1910, Texans were flying airplanes.

Texas and Texans were ready for the 20th Century.

In Galveston alone, six thousand
Felt the hand of death,
While twenty towns were withered
By the cyclone's cruel breath.
Excerpt from THE GALVESTON STORM

The Bishop's Palace, Galveston.

THE STATE CAPITOL

By the end of the century, Texas could boast the largest state capital building in the United States.

It was built by a group of Illinois businessmen in exchange for three million acres of state land in the Panhandle. Modeled after the national capitol in Washington, it was to have been constructed of native limestone from quarries near Austin; but someone discovered that the "fool's gold" in the stone would cause rusty streaks—so pink Texas granite was used instead.

The magnificent building was officially opened in 1888. It rises three hundred feet from the ground to the top of the figure of justice above the dome.

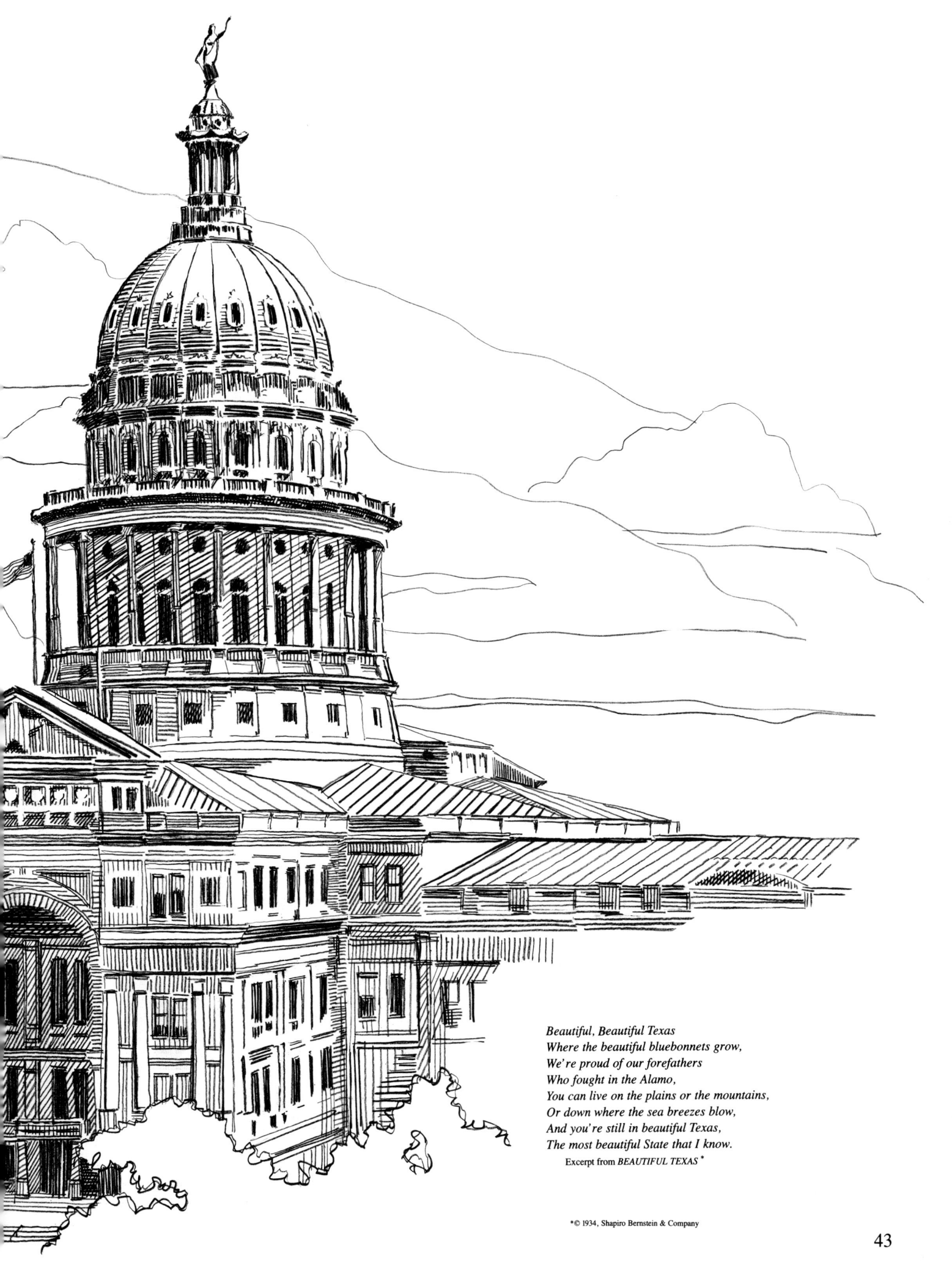

Beautiful, Beautiful Texas
Where the beautiful bluebonnets grow,
We're proud of our forefathers
Who fought in the Alamo,
You can live on the plains or the mountains,
Or down where the sea breezes blow,
And you're still in beautiful Texas,
The most beautiful State that I know.
  Excerpt from *BEAUTIFUL TEXAS* *

* © 1934, Shapiro Bernstein & Company

WORLD WAR I

After it became a state, Texas continued to have trouble on the Rio Grande border. Raids by Mexican bandits and revolutionaries were common, but now came another and graver threat.

Europe had been at war since 1914. The United States had remained neutral, but in 1917 a secret telegram from the German Foreign Secretary to the German Minister in Mexico was intercepted by British Intelligence. Once decoded, the telegram revealed that Germany was urging Mexico to declare war on the United States. After winning the war, Germany would then return Texas and other lands to Mexico. President Woodrow Wilson published the telegram, and five weeks later the United States declared war on Germany.

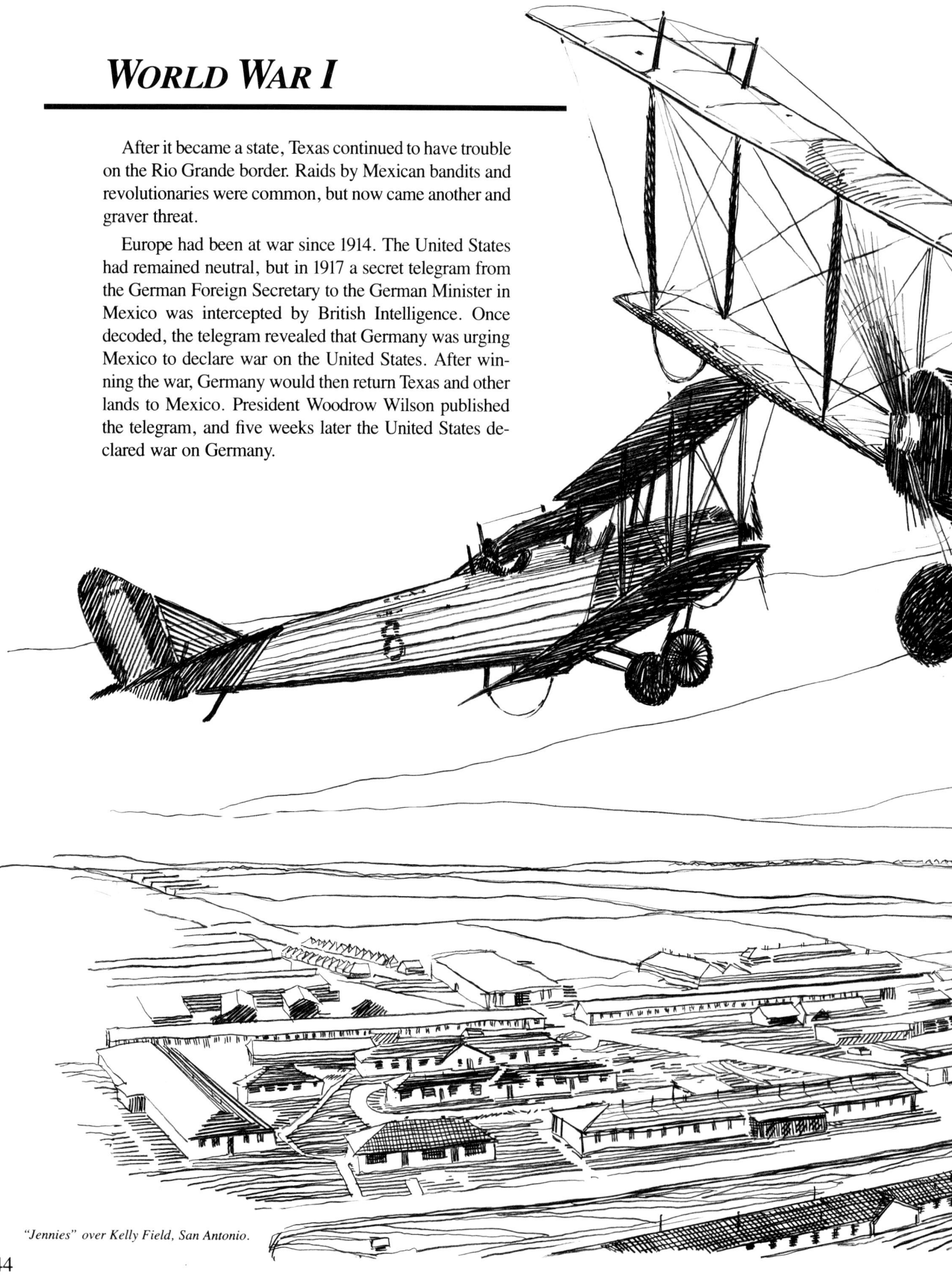

"Jennies" over Kelly Field, San Antonio.

Texans rallied to the cause. Troops were stationed on the Mexican border and training camps established throughout the state. Texans were urged to "Give Till It Hurts" and "Buy More Bonds"... and all over the state you could hear the rousing words of "Over There".

Over there, over there, send the word, send the word over there.
That the Yanks are coming, the Yanks are coming,
The drum's rum-tumming everywhere.
Excerpt from *OVER THERE* *

*© renewed 1945. CBS Songs.

OIL BOOM

The first oil strikes were made by the Indians who bathed in the oil springs to cure skin diseases, rheumatism, and sores. They also used oil on cuts and burns, and some Indians even drank the stuff.

The explorers and early settlers used the black seepage to caulk boats and to grease the axles of carts and wagons, but Spindletop changed the face of Texas. It created boom towns—just as the gold rush had done in California.

The East Texas oil strike in the 1930's was one of the biggest ever. Promoters, speculators, wildcatters, and even tourists flooded the strike areas. Rooms rented by the hour. Food and supplies doubled in price. The streets were crowded and rutted by the heavy traffic. Wooden derricks went up; and drillers, roustabouts, tool dressers . . . practically everyone dreamed of striking it rich.

A new Texas legend was born.

O, the toolie of a drilling crew
With short and feverish breath,
In a boarding house in Beaumont,
Lay near the point of death.
Excerpt from THE DYING TOOLIE

Burkburnett, 1918.

WORLD WAR II

By the late 1930's war was breaking out again in Europe and Asia. At first the United States tried to remain neutral; but with the massive Japanese attack on Pearl Harbor in 1941, America went to war too.

Training camps were established on Texas soil. The 36th Division—often called the Texas army because so many Texans served in it—fought through Europe, carrying the Lone Star flag and Old Glory side by side all the way. Inside the staff of the Texas flag was a copy of Travis' letter at the Alamo; and it was said, each man knew that letter by heart.

The Battleship Texas.

The stars at night are big and bright
(clap, clap, clap, clap)
Deep in the heart of Texas . . .
The prairie sky is wide and high
(clap, clap, clap, clap)
Deep in the heart of Texas . . .
Excerpt from DEEP IN THE HEART OF TEXAS *

In the bloody but decisive D-Day invasion of 1944, the Battleship *Texas* served as the fleet flagship. The invasion was commanded by General Dwight D. Eisenhower, born in Denison, Texas, and destined to become the Supreme Allied Commander in Europe, and then president of the United States.

Texans fought valiantly in the war. A native Texan became the most decorated soldier in the Army, and another Texan was honored by being the most decorated sailor in the Navy.

*© 1941, Melody Lane Publications, Inc.

MODERN TEXAS

After the war, Texas prospered and forged new frontiers. She became an industrial and commercial center. She pioneered in medicine and in space. She sent another native son, Lyndon Baines Johnson, to the White House. She has survived economic booms and busts—her cities continue to flourish—and Texas goes from strength to strength.

The people keep coming, just as they did in the days of Stephen F. Austin. From all over, the modern settlers still come—to this land of stark contrasts, great natural treasures, and a rich heritage drawn from many cultures and languages.

The tall tales and legends are more than fancies of the imagination. They come from history—history hard-won and hard-lived.

They come from TEXAS!

Dallas skyline.

SPACE

THE NEW FRONTIER

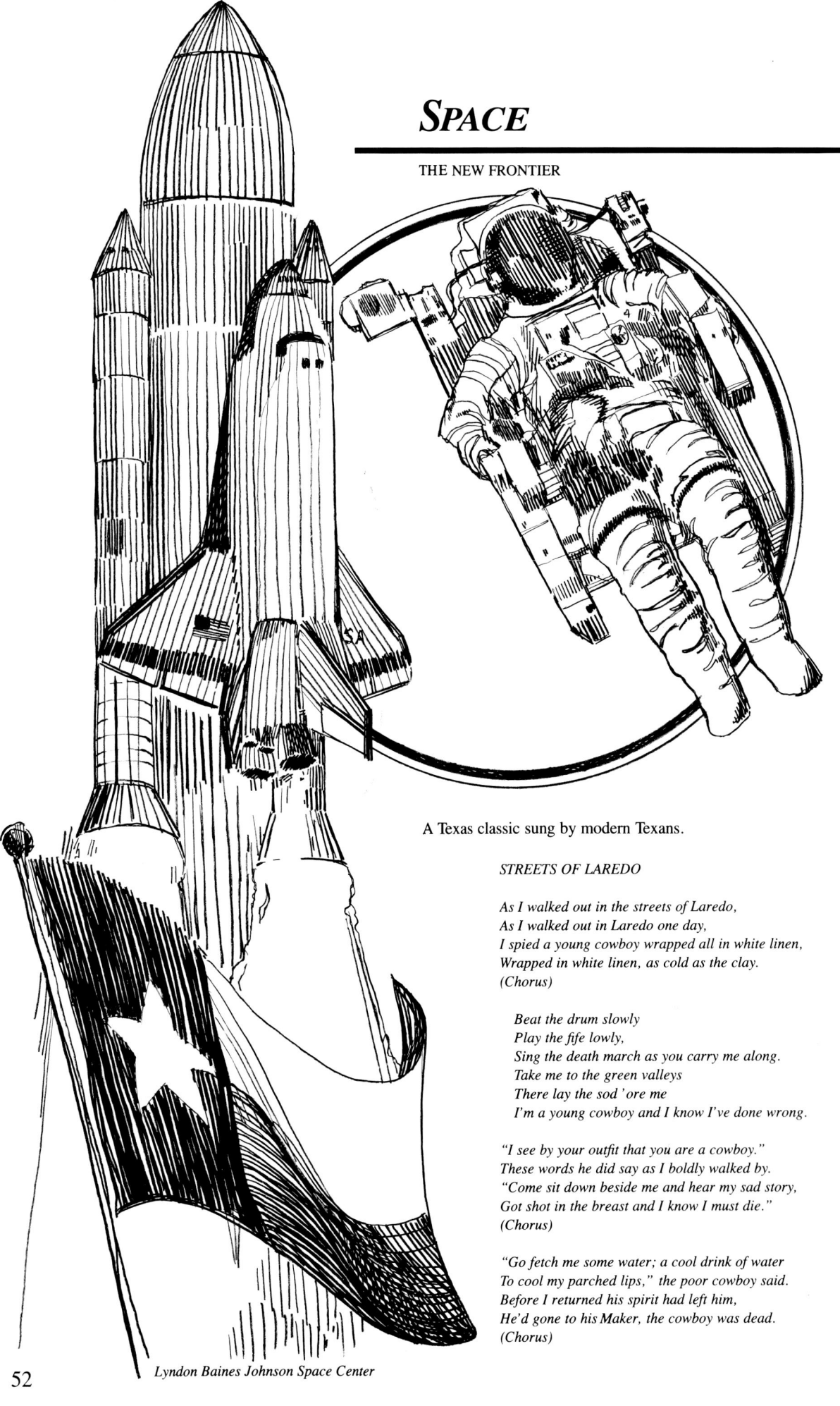

Lyndon Baines Johnson Space Center

A Texas classic sung by modern Texans.

STREETS OF LAREDO

*As I walked out in the streets of Laredo,
As I walked out in Laredo one day,
I spied a young cowboy wrapped all in white linen,
Wrapped in white linen, as cold as the clay.
(Chorus)*

   *Beat the drum slowly
   Play the fife lowly,
   Sing the death march as you carry me along.
   Take me to the green valleys
   There lay the sod 'ore me
   I'm a young cowboy and I know I've done wrong.*

*"I see by your outfit that you are a cowboy."
These words he did say as I boldly walked by.
"Come sit down beside me and hear my sad story,
Got shot in the breast and I know I must die."
(Chorus)*

*"Go fetch me some water; a cool drink of water
To cool my parched lips," the poor cowboy said.
Before I returned his spirit had left him,
He'd gone to his Maker, the cowboy was dead.
(Chorus)*

THE SONGS OF TEXAS

These are the songs Texans sang—and to which they marched, danced, rocked their children, toiled, and died—during the very period of history that each was sung.

FLAG SONG . . . Caddo Indian tribal song

The music of the Indians arises from nature itself. The beat of the drum is as constant as the beat of the heart, and the melodies are repeated again and again as a bird call might be.

Many Indian myths say that the Creator sang life into being—even as the Creator in Genesis speaks life into being. All of their songs are not religious, but all of them are said to carry a spiritual power which is felt to miscarry if the song is not performed with accuracy.

Flag Song is the Caddo National Anthem. It is sung before "powwows" (tribal councils) or when warriors are going off to battle, just as "The Star Spangled Banner" is sung.

TURKEY DANCE . . . Caddo Indian Dance
(Indians, pp. 10 and 11)

Indian dances often imitate the movements of birds or animals and are named for them. The dancers might admire the great strength or endurance or courage of the buffalo, for instance, and imitate the creature in hope of attracting these qualities to themselves.

The Turkey Dance is an early afternoon dance which starts between 3:00 and 5:00 p.m. and lasts until sunset. The dance is mainly a women's dance, but there is a section of the activity which resembles the courtship of the bird itself—where the women chase down partners and the couples dance together for a while. A special hair ornament is worn by the women (for this dance only), perhaps because of the ancient courtship nature of the activity.

CADDO FLAG SONG

Listen all you people!
We are taking down the flag!
Wherever our warriors are . . .
On distant battlefields . . .
May they return safely!

CIELITO LINDO
(The Spanish, pp. 12 and 13)

There was a sharp contrast between the music of the Indians (some of whom were still indulging in ritual cannibalism when the Spanish landed) and the music of the Spanish invaders (who were said to be debating the merits of traditional Roman Catholic church music as compared to the music ushered in by the Reformation).

Cielito Lindo is a simple folk song, but it does show the subtleties of the more advanced Spanish culture.

CIELITO LINDO	(English translation)
De la Sierra Morena, Cielito Lindo, vienen bajando Un par de ojitos negros, Cielito Lindo, de contrabando.	*From the Sierra Morena, Cielito Lindo, there are coming down A pair of black eyes, Cielito Lindo, stealthily.*
(Chorus) *Ay, ay, ay, ay* *Canta y no llores* *Porque cantando se alegran, Cielito Lindo, los corazones.*	*(Chorus)* *Ay, ay, ay, ay* *Sing and don't cry* *Because singing, Cielito Lindo, makes the hearts happy.*
Ay, ay, ay, ay *Canta y no llores* *Porque cantando se alegran, Cielito Lindo, los corazones.*	*Ay, ay, ay, ay* *Sing and don't cry,* *Because singing, Cielito Lindo, makes the hearts happy.*
Una flecha en el aire, Cielito Lindo, lanzó Cupido *Y como fué jugando, Cielito Lindo, yo fuí el herido.* *(Chorus)*	*An arrow in the air, Cielito Lindo, Cupid threw,* *And as I was playing, Cielito Lindo, I was wounded.* *(Chorus)*

AU CLAIR DE LA LUNE
(The French, p. 14)

As in many of Shakespeare's sonnets, this old French folk song leans very heavily on the double *entendre*—i.e., a word or expression capable of two interpretations, one of them often being risqué.

AU CLAIR DE LA LUNE	(English Translation)
Au clair de la lune *Mon ami Pierrot,* *Prête-moi ta plume* *Pour écrire un mot;* *Ma chandelle est morte,* *Je n'ai plus de feu;* *Ouvre-moi ta porte* *Pour l'amour de Dieu.*	*By the light of the moon* *My friend Pierrot,* *I take my pen* *To write a word;* *My candle is dead,* *I have no more fire;* *Open your door to me* *For the love of God.*

LIBERA ME . . . Gregorian Chant
(Spanish Missions, p. 15)

As Christianity spread from Judea to be the accepted faith of the civilized western world, it brought with it its own mixture of music—partly Jewish chant and partly borrowed melodies from Classical Greece and Imperial Rome.

In about A.D. 600 Pope Gregory the Great determined to develop a system of notation for the varieties of musical scales used in Christian church music. They became known as Gregorian modes and were used extensively in the Roman Catholic service of worship. A style of plainsong survives today bearing his name.

LIBERA ME

Libera me, Domine, de morte æterna
In die illa tremenda:
Quando cæli movendi sunt et terra:
Dum veneris judicare sæculum per ignem.

(English translation)
Deliver me, O Lord, from eternal death
On that awesome day:
When the Heavens and the earth shall shake
When Thou comest to judge the world with fire.

INDIAN WAR DANCE . . . Plains Indians

The *War Dance* was performed as a ceremony to prepare warriors for battle. Usually a post—seven or eight feet high—was set up in the center of the village. Sometimes the post was painted or peeled, and sometimes it had a roasted dog at its foot. When the chief wanted to raise a war party, he began by striking the post with a club or tomahawk and reciting his brave deeds against the enemy. Other warriors would come forward, strike the post and recite their brave deeds. If the roasted dog was a part of the ceremony, those assembled would then eat the dog—but would keep walking around showing that they were always on guard. The music had little melody, and the ceremony was conducted with the seriousness of performing an important public duty.

SIOUX INDIANS . . . A Settlers' Song
(Indians on Horseback, pp. 16 and 17)

Here, where the settlers' songs meet the music of the Indians, we realize the bitter conflict in which both of these groups find themselves. *Sioux Indians* is one of the greatest of the overlanders' ballads and gives in detail the settlers' view of the dilemma.

SHOOT THE BUFFALO
(Anglo-American Settlers, p. 18)

As the first Anglo-Americans made their way into Texas, they brought with them a new form of expression—the play-party. In East Texas they were called "Josey" parties and in other parts of the United States were known as ring game parties. They were akin to the singing games played in England, but the music was purely frontier.

The music was sung by a caller (as in square dancing) and by those who were dancing. The activity was not called dancing because many religious groups disapproved of dancing. Many also felt that musical instruments were not a part of the New Testament revelation of the Gospel—especially the fiddle, which was considered to be the devil's instrument.

Play-parties were usually held in the winter—leaving the summer free for religious revivals and camp meetings—and seemed to allow for courting among the young people without raising undo criticism from their elders.

SIOUX INDIANS

I'll sing you a song, though it may be a sad one,
Of trials and troubles and where first begun.
I left my dear kindred, my friends, and my home,
And we crossed the wide deserts and mountains to roam.

While taking refreshments we heard a low yell,
The whoop of Sioux Indians coming up from the dell;
We sprang to our rifles with a flash in each eye.
"Boys," says our brave leader, "we'll fight till we die."

They made a bold dash and came near to our train,
And the arrows fell round us like hail and like rain;
But with our long rifles we fed them cold lead,
Till many a brave warrior around us lay dead.

With our small band there were just twenty-four,
And the Sioux Indians there were five hundred or more;
We fought them with courage; we spoke not a word,
Till the end of the battle was all that was heard.

We shot their bold chief at the head of his band;
He died like a warrior with a gun in his hand.
When they saw their bold chief lying dead in his gore,
They whooped and they yelled, and we saw them no more.

We hitched up our horses and started our train;
Three more bloody battles this trip on the plain;
And in our last battle three of our brave boys fell,
And we left them to rest in a green shady dell.

SHOOT THE BUFFALO

Rise you up, my partner dear,
And present to me your hand,
'Cause I know you want to marry,
And I'd like to be the man.
And I'll take you out to Texas,
Where I know you want to go,
And we'll rally round the canebrake,
And shoot the buffalo.

(Chorus)
Shoot the buffalo,
We will shoot the buffalo,
We'll ramble through the canebrake,
And shoot the buffalo.

Rise you up, my partner dear,
And present to me your hand,
And we'll take a little journey
To a fair and distant land.
Where the boys will scrap and rassle,
And the girls will sit and sew,
And we'll rally round the canebrake,
And shoot the buffalo.
(Chorus)

Well the buffalo is dead;
We've done shot him in the head,
So let's all form a circle,
And we'll have a dance instead.
And the hawk will chase the buzzard,
And the buzzard chase the crow,
And we'll rally round the canebrake,
And shoot the buffalo.
(Chorus)

CAPTAIN KIDD
(Filibusters and Pirates, p. 19)

Nautical ballads told of gales, and wrecks, of sea-fights and the men-before-the-mast. "Captain Kid's Farewel to the Seas" was the original name for the song *Captain Kidd*. It was one of the newer pirate songs which began around the first part of the eighteenth century. These featured the eastern seas rather than the Spanish Main or Barbary Coast.

Captain Kidd had settled in New York and was commissioned to sail as a privateer for the King of England against the pirates and French ships sacking the British ships at sea. When prizes became scarce he turned to outright piracy with great success. After returning to Gardiner's Island—which lies at the eastern tip of Long Island—he was arrested, returned to London, and hanged on Execution Dock in 1701. Part of his buried booty was recovered from Gardiner's Island in 1699. The remainder has never been found.

CAPTAIN KIDD

Oh my name is Captain Kidd, as I sailed, as I sailed,
My name is Captain Kidd, as I sailed;
My name is Captain Kidd, God's laws I did forbid,
And most wickedly I did, as I sailed, as I sailed.

Oh, I steered from sound to sound, as I sailed, as I sailed,
I steered from sound to sound, and many ships I found,
And all of them I burned, as I sailed, as I sailed.

And being cruel still, as I sailed, as I sailed,
And being cruel still, my gunner I did kill,
And his precious blood did spill, as I sailed, as I sailed.

I was sick and nigh to death, as I sailed, as I sailed,
I was sick and nigh to death and I vowed with every breath,
To walk in wisdom's ways, when I sailed, when I sailed.

My repentance lasted not, as I sailed, as I sailed,
My repentance lasted not, my vows I soon forgot,
Damnation was my lot, as I sailed, as I sailed.

To the execution dock I must go, I must go,
To the execution dock, while many thousands flock,
But I must bear the shock and must die, and must die.

Take a warning now by me, for I must die, for I must die,
Take a warning now by me and shun bad company,
Lest you come to hell with me, for I must die, I must die.

TEXAS BOYS
(The Old Three Hundred, p. 20)

Not everyone thought their daughters should venture into the wilds of Texas—especially the mothers living in the more settled neighboring states. Above all they felt that the girls should stay away from the boys who would take them there.

Texas Boys is in the category known as the "come-all-ye" folk song—which is designed to give the foolish the benefit of some sage advice.

TEXAS BOYS

Come all you young ladies and listen to my noise,
And don't you go marrying those Texas boys,
'Cause if you do your life's gonna be
Johnnycake and venison and sassafras tea,
Johnnycake and venison and sassafras tea.

When they come a-courtin' I'll tell you what they wear,
An old tattered shirt all patched and bare,
An old straw hat more brim than crown,
And a pair of leather britches that they wear the winter round,
A pair of leather britches that they wear the winter round.

They'll take you out to some lone pine hill,
And leave you to starve against your will,
They'll leave you alone out there in the sand,
And that is the way with a Tex-i-an,
That is the way with a Tex-i-an.

So candy's candy any way you fix it,
Brandy's brandy any way you mix it.
When other good folks are asleep in bed,
The devil is a-workin' in a Texan's head,
The devil is a-workin' in a Texan's head.

Sassafras

EL RANCHO GRANDE
(Mexican Rule, p. 21)

The Mexican cattle kingdom helped to establish the Mexican culture in Texas. *El Rancho Grande* is a ranch song which is a favorite among Mexican citizens and Texans alike. The *vaquero* (Mexican cowboy) tells of his sweetheart who gives us some insight into the apparel of the *vaquero* . . . i.e., wool trousers finished with leather. A large *sombrero* and a brightly colored shawl or wrap called a *serape* also form a part of this uniform.

EL RANCHO GRANDE (Mexican)

*Allá en el rancho grande,
allá donde vivía
había una rancherita
que alegre me decía
que alegre me decía,*

*"Te voy a hacer tus calzones
como los que usa el ranchero
te los comienzo de lana
y los acabo de cuero."*

*El gusto de los ranchero
es tener su buen caballo
ensillarlo por la tarde
y darle vuelta al potrero.*

(English translation)

*Down there at the big ranch,
down there where I lived,
there was a little maid
who gaily said to me;*

*"I am going to make you some trousers
like those worn by the ranchmen.
I shall begin them with wool
but finish them in leather."*

*The greatest joy of the ranchmen
is to have a good horse,
to saddle him in the afternoon
and go out to see the pastures.*

THE GAL I LEFT BEHIND ME
(Texas Volunteers, pp. 22 and 23)

The Gal I Left Behind Me was popular in Elizabethan England as a fife song and in Colonial America as a stage song. Its origins are probably Irish or a melody adapted from a British song named "Brighton Camp." It was also played on the docks as a salute to warships leaving the harbor; as a play-party song; and as a farewell song sung by men marching off to war.

THE GAL I LEFT BEHIND ME

*I'm lonesome since I crossed the hills
And o'er the moor and valley;
Such heavy thoughts my heart does fill
Since parting with my Sally.*

*I seek no more the young and gay
For each does but remind me
Of that gal, that pretty little gal,
The gal I left behind me.*

*(Chorus)
O that gal, that pretty little gal,
The gal I left behind me;
I'm going to stop and stay all night
With the gal I left behind me.*

*If ever I travel this road again
And the angels they don't find me,
I'll make my way back home again
To the gal I left behind me.*

*I'll cross Red River one more time
If the tears don't fall and drown me,
I'll reconcile and stay a while
With the gal I left behind me.*

(Chorus)

Wild Rose

COME TO THE BOWER
(The Revolution, pp. 24 and 25)

Texas legend has it that *Come to the Bower* was sung by Davy Crockett at the Alamo; but better documentation supports the tradition that the Texas army marched into battle at San Jacinto to this song.

COME TO THE BOWER

*Will you come to the bower I have shaded for you?
I have decked it with roses all spangled with dew.
Will you, will you, will you, will you, Come to my bower?
Will you, will you, will you, will you, Come to my bower?*

*There beneath this glad bower on roses you'll rest,
While a smile lights the eyes of the girl I love best.
Will you, will you, will you, will you, Come to my bower?
Will you, will you, will you, will you, Come to my bower?*

*We shall swear 'mid the roses we never shall part,
O thou fairest of roses, thou queen of my heart.
Will you, will you, will you, will you, Come to my bower?
Will you, will you, will you, will you, Come to my bower?*

57

TEXAS HEROES
(The Republic of Texas, p. 26)

Texas Heroes, sung to the tune of the old Scots folk song, "Auld Lang Syne," is one of our oldest patriotic songs. It became popular soon after the battle of San Jacinto and was sung every San Jacinto Day for years.

One of the locations where the song must have been sung with great reverence was around the twenty foot high "Liberty Pole" which had been erected by the veterans of the battle of San Jacinto. It was used as a flag pole from which the Lone Star flag flew on festive occasions—and certainly on San Jacinto Day.

The pole, which had been a rallying point for the veterans for years, finally rotted and was taken down by the veterans themselves. It was not retired without the proper salute, however, which was by the firing of the "Twin Sisters" (the two brass cannons used by Texans to win their independence).

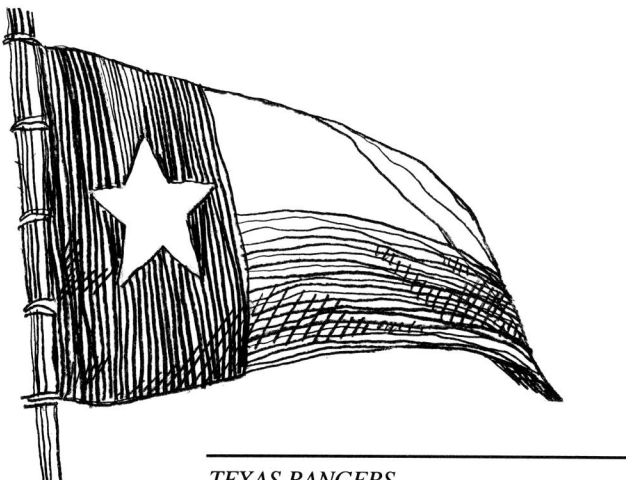

TEXAS HEROES

We lay the crown of memory
Upon the place of rest
Where noble heroes lie asleep
Within Earth's icy breast.

(Chorus)
Then strike the harp for those who fought
For freedom long ago,
At San Jacinto and the Mier
And blood-stained Alamo.

For those who fell at Alamo,
And those who died at Mier,
And those brave hearts still at Goliad,
All claim the silent tear.
(Chorus)

On San Jacinto's crimson plain
Brave Houston met the foe,
And set his sturdy heel upon
The chief of Mexico.
(Chorus)

When Santa Anna's star went down,
The Lone Star rose on high,
And blazed aloft a brilliant light
In freedom's cloudless sky.
(Chorus)

For those who wear upon the brow
The crown of honored years,
And those who bravely died we offer
A chaplet of our tears.
(Chorus)

TEXAS RANGERS
(Texas Rangers, p. 27)

Although a great frontier ballad, *Texas Rangers* retains some elements of its ancestry—a British stall ballad.

The stall ballads were entertainment for the general public. Usually printed in old black letter type, they were sold from stalls (or booths) by those who could sing, play, and also hawk their wares.

Those creating the songs would often simply find a piece of poetry, choose a suitable tune, and then put the two together. The themes of the ballads were universal; but many were also current, i.e., expanding upon whatever story was headlining the news and in whatever style was popular with the people (such as rock and roll, rhythm and blues, or country-western might be today).

TEXAS RANGERS

Come all you Texas Rangers
Where ever you may be,
I will tell you of some trouble
That happened unto me.

My name is nothing extra
Of that I will not tell.
But first to all the Rangers
I want to wish them well.

At the age of seventeen
I joined the Jolly Band
We marched from San Antonio
Out to the Rio Grande.

Our captain, he informed us
Perhaps he thought it right,
Before we reached the station
Says he, "We'll have to fight."

We saw the Indians coming.
We heard them give the yell.
My thoughts at that moment,
No tongue could ever tell.

I thought then of my mother
At home to me did say,
"To you, they all are strangers,
With me, you had better stay,"

I knew that she was childish,
The best she did not know,
My mind was bent on roving,
And I was sure to go.

We fought a full nine hours
Before the strife was over,
The like of dead and wounded
You never saw before.

There was nine as noble Rangers
As ever saw the West
Was buried beside their comrades
And there to take their rest.

SOMETIMES I FEEL LIKE A MOTHERLESS CHILE
(Statehood, pp. 28 and 29)

So many of our Afro-American Texans came from the west coast of Africa; and their memories, traditions, language, and music were about all that they could bring with them. Many of the Black folk songs seem to be altered versions of very old songs. They were handed down orally and the words changed to suit whatever situations the singer was facing in everyday life.

Sometimes I Feel Like a Motherless Chile rings with the experience of a human being who indeed has been separated from mother, father, spouse, and children—separated from his or her very identity.

MUSS I DENN

If the Afro-American Texans were unable to bring much of their homeland with them, the German Texans were able to transport a great deal of their cultural heritage to the new land. Bringing songbooks and instruments, they quickly formed singing clubs and bands. Often these singing clubs became the nuclei of social activities in the German settlements—so important was music to their lives. *Muss i Denn* is a great favorite. German Texans recount the story of boatloads of immigrants sailing out of Bremen harbor as brass bands played *Muss i Denn*. These same ships were met on the docks at Galveston by bands playing the same song.

SOMETIMES I FEEL LIKE A MOTHERLESS CHILE

Sometimes I feel like a motherless chile,
Sometimes I feel like a motherless chile,
Sometimes I feel like a motherless chile,
Far, far away from home,
A long, long ways from home.

Sometimes I feel like I'm almost gone,
Sometimes I feel like I'm almost gone,
Sometimes I feel like I'm almost gone,
Far, far away from home,
A long, long ways from home.

MUSS I DENN

Muss i denn, muss i denn
Zum Städtele hinaus, Städtele hinaus,
Und du, mei Schatz, bleibst hier?
Wenn i komm, wenn i komm,
Wenn i wiederum komm, wiederum komm,
Kehr i ein, mei Schatz, dei dir.
Kann i gleich nit allweil bei dir sein,
Han i doch mei Freud an dir.
Wenn i komm, wenn i komm,
Wenn i wiederum komm, wiederum komm,
Kehr i ein, mei Schatz, bei dir.

Wie du weinst, wei du weinst,
Dass i wandere muss, wandere muss,
Wie, wenn d'Lieb' jetzt wär vorbei!
Sind au drauss, sind au drauss
Der Mädele viel, Mädele viel,
Lieber Schatz, i bleib dir treu.
Denk du nit, wenn i ein andre seh,
So sei mei Lieb vorbei.
Sind au drauss, sind au drauss
Der Mädele viel, Mädele viel,
Lieber Schatz, i bleib dir treu.

(English translation)

Must I then, must I then
From my town go away, town go away,
And you, my love, stay here?
When I come, when I come,
When I come back again, come back again,
I will come to you, my dear.
Though I can't be with you all the time,
I still love you, my dear.
When I come, when I come,
When I come back again, come back again,
I will come to you, my dear.

How you cry, how you cry
That I must go away, must go away,
As though our love were past,
In the world, in the world
Many gals may be, gals may be,
Dear heart, I will stay true.
Don't think when other girls I see
That our love will go away,
In the world, in the world
Many gals may be, gals may be,
Dear heart, I will stay true.

DIXIE
(The Civil War, pp. 30 and 31)

Daniel Emmett's *Dixie*, which was written in 1859, was a "hurrah" song or a "walk-around" in Jerry Bryant's minstrel show. One legend has it that the song was named for the "Dix" (which was a ten dollar bill that was issued before 1860 by the Citizen's Bank of New Orleans). The bill eventually became known as a "dixie," and Northerners would say: "I'm going down to 'Dixie's Land' "—meaning the South.

Another explanation was printed in an old (undated) newspaper article: "Dixie owned a tract of land on Manhattan Island and also a large number of slaves; and his slaves increasing faster than his land, an emigration ensued . . . The negroes who left it for different parts looked to it as a place of unalloyed happiness . . . Hence Dixie became synonymous with an ideal locality . . . 'Dixie Land' has become very popular in our section since the election of Lincoln, and has almost entirely superceded 'Yankee Doodle.' It will doubtless be adopted as the national air of the Southern Confederacy."

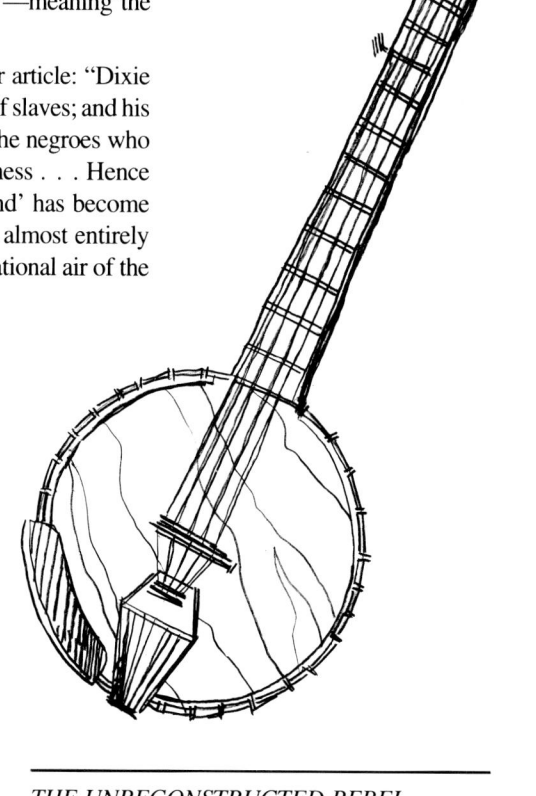

DIXIE'S LAND

I wish I was in de land of cotton,
Old times dar am not forgotten;
Look away! Look away! Look away! Dixie Land.
In Dixie Land whar I was born in,
Early on one frosty mornin',
Look away! Look away! Look away! Dixie Land.

(Chorus)
Den I wish I was in Dixie, hooray! hooray!
In Dixie Land I'll take my stand
To lib an' die in Dixie, away! away!
Away down South in Dixie, away! away!
Away down South in Dixie.

THE YELLOW ROSE OF TEXAS

Like "Dixie," *The Yellow Rose of Texas* was a favorite marching song of Hood's Texas Brigade.

THE YELLOW ROSE OF TEXAS

There's a Yellow Rose in Texas, that I am going to see,
No other soldier knows her, no one but only me;
She cried so when I left her, it like to broke my heart,
And if I ever find her, we nevermore will part.

(Chorus)
She's the sweetest little flower this soldier ever knew,
Her eyes are bright as diamonds, they sparkle like the dew;
You may talk about your Dearest May and sing of Rosa Lee,
But the Yellow Rose of Texas is the only rose for me.

When the Rio Grande is flowing, and the starry skies are bright,
She walks along the river in the quiet summer night;
She thinks if I remember, when we parted long ago,
I promised to come back again, and not to leave her so.
(Chorus)

O now I'm going to find her, for my heart is full of woe,
And we'll sing the songs together, that we sang so long ago.
We'll play the banjo gaily, and we'll sing the songs of yore,
And the Yellow Rose of Texas shall be mine forevermore.
(Chorus)

THE UNRECONSTRUCTED REBEL
(Reconstruction, pp. 32 and 33)

The Unreconstructed Rebel is a true Reconstruction song. Life was very difficult for most Texans after the Civil War; and in the Texas spirit, they did not "take it" lying down.

GOOD OLD REBEL
or
THE UNRECONSTRUCTED REBEL

Oh, I'm a good old Rebel,
Yes, that is what I am.
For this fair land of freedom
I do not give a dram.
I'm glad I fought against it;
I only wish we'd won,
And I don't want no pardon
For anything I've done.

I hate the Constitution,
This Great Republic too.
I hate the Freedmen's Bureau
And uniform of blue.
I hate the nasty eagle
With all its brag and fuss,
But the lyin', thievin' Yankees
I hate 'em wuss and wuss!

I followed old Marse Robert
Three year or nigh about,
Got wounded in three places
And starved at P'int Lookout.
I cotch the rheumatism
A-camping in the snow,
But I killed a mess of Yankees
And I'd like to kill some more.

I can't take up my musket
And fight 'em now no more,
And I ain't going to love 'em
And that is certain shore,
And I don't want no pardon
For what I done or am,
And I won't be reconstructed
And I don't gave a dram!

THE GREER COUNTY BACHELOR
(Trails West, pp. 34 and 35)

There is an underlying cheer about *The Greer County Bachelor*. Sung to the tune of the "Irish Washerwoman," the song is set in old Greer County, Texas—which later became a part of Oklahoma. Beneath the cheer we are faced with the realities of frontier life. The song is a classic in that it lists so many of the hardships these settlers had to face while trying to hold down their claims.

THE GREER COUNTY BACHELOR

My name is Tom Hight; an old bachelor I am;
You'll find me out west in the country of fame,
You'll find me out west on an elegant plan,
Just a-starving to death on my government claim.

(Chorus)
Hurrah, for Greer County! The land of the free,
The land of the grasshopper, bedbug, and flea!
I'll sing of its praises and tell of its fame
And starve plumb to death on my government claim.

My house it is built out of natural soil,
The walls are erected according to Hoyle,
Its roof has no pitch and is level and plain,
And I always get wet when it happens to rain.
(Chorus)

My clothes are all ragged; my language is rough,
My bread is corn dodgers, both solid and tough,
And yet I am happy and live at my ease
On sorghum molasses and bacon and cheese.
(Chorus)

How happy am I when I crawl into bed,
And a rattlesnake hisses a tune at my head,
A gay little centipede, all without fear,
Crawls over my pillow and into my ear.
(Chorus)

Now come all you claim holders, and I hope you will stay
To chew your hardtack till you're toothless and gray,
But as for me I'll no longer remain,
To starve like a dog on my government claim.
(Chorus)

Farewell to Greer County where the buzzards arise,
Where the sun never sets and the flea never dies,
Where the wind never ceases but always remains
To blow us all off of our government claims.

THE BUFFALO HUNTERS
(The Buffalo Hunters, p. 36)

Carl Sandburg thought that *The Buffalo Hunters* was one of America's finest folk songs and actually sang it on his speaking tours across the country. In his 1927 book, *The American Songbag*, he says that the song is a "magnificent find . . . the framework of a big, sweeping novel of real life condensed into a few stanzas."

The tune began as a love song called "Caldonia," then became an English sea chantey (a sailors' song usually sung to the rhythm of work), and later was sung as a far-north logging song—before making its way to Texas.

THE BUFFALO HUNTERS

'Twas in the town of Jacksboro in the spring of 'seventy-three,
A man by the name of Crego came stepping up to me,
Saying, "How do you do, young fellow, and how would you like to go
And spend one summer pleasantly on the range of the buffalo?"

It's me being out of employment, to Crego I did say,
"This going out on the buffalo range depends upon the pay,
But if you pay good wages and transportation, too,
Well, sir, I will go with you to the range of the buffalo."

So now our outfit was complete, seven able-bodied men.
With navy six and needle gun our troubles did begin;
Our way it was a pleasant one, the route we had to go,
Until we crossed Pease River on the range of the buffalo.

He fed us on such sorry chuck I wished myself most dead,
And all we had to sleep on was a buffalo robe for a bed;
The fleas and graybacks worked on us, O boys, it was not slow;
There's no worse life on this old earth than the range of the buffalo.

Our hearts were cased with buffalo hocks, our souls were cased with steel,
And the hardships of that summer would nearly make us reel.
While skinning the durn old stinkers our lives they had no show,
For the Indians waited to pick us off on the range of the buffalo.

The season being over, old Crego he did say
The crowd had been extravagant, was in debt to him that day,
We coaxed him and we begged him and still it was no go—
So we left old Crego's bones to bleach on the range of the buffalo.

Oh, it's now we've crossed Pease River and homeward we are bound,
No more in that hell-fired country shall ever we be found;
Go home to our wives and sweethearts, tell others not to go,
For God's forsaken the buffalo range and the durn old buffalo.

GIT ALONG, LITTLE DOGIES
(The Cowboy and the Cattle Kingdom, p. 37)

During the long night watches on the trail, the cowboys often sang to the cattle to calm them. *Git Along, Little Dogies* is a cowboy lullaby derived from an old Irish lullaby called "The Old Man Rocking the Cradle."

The "dogie" is a little calf that has lost its mother before it is ready to be weaned. Its digestive system has not developed enough to handle grass well, and therefore its stomach bloats. The cowboys would say that the calf's gut was full of dough, or a "dough-gut." The name finally became shortened into "dogie."

GIT ALONG, LITTLE DOGIES

As I was out walking one morning for pleasure,
I spied a cowpuncher a-riding along;
His hat was throwed back and his spurs were a-jingling,
And as he approached he was singing this song.

(Chorus)
Whoopee ti yi yo, git along, little dogies,
It's your misfortune and none of my own;
Whoopee ti yi yo, git along, little dogies,
For you know that Wyoming will be your new home.

It's early in springtime we're rounding up dogies,
Roping and branding and bobbing their tails,
Whooping and yelling, "Git along, little dogies,"
And pushing them out on the old Chisholm Trail.
(Chorus)

You're going to be soup for Uncle Sam's Indians,
It's "Beef, heap beef!" I still hear them cry.
So get up, get up, get along, little dogies,
You're going to be beefsteak in the sweet bye and bye.
(Chorus)

THE WABASH CANNONBALL
(Railroads, p. 38)

As locomotive transportation flourished so did a new rhythm and tempo in music—giving rise to railroad songs. Many of these songs were written by those riding closest to the rails—the hoboes.

The train, the Wabash Cannonball, was to hoboes what the "Flying Dutchman" was to sailors. It was a mystical train that supposedly had seven hundred cars—ran everywhere—rode on a railroad whose ties were made of entire redwood trees—moved so fast that even when it stopped it was still going 65 miles an hour—with a conductor who punched tickets by shooting holes in them with a .45 caliber automatic.

WABASH CANNONBALL

Listen to the jingle, the rumble and the roar,
As it glides along the woodlands, by the hills, and by the shore.
Hear the mighty rush of the engine; hear the lonesome lobo squall;
We're flying through the jungle on the Wabash Cannonball.

She came down to Birmingham one cold December day,
As she pulled into the station, you could hear the people say,
"There's a gal from Alabam, she's long and she's tall,
And she's come down to Birmingham on the Wabash Cannonball."

Now here's to Daddy Claxton, may his name forever stand,
He's a brakeman that's respected by the hoboes in the land;
And when his days are over and the curtains round him fall,
May his spirit ever linger on the Wabash Cannonball.

ROSEWOOD CASKET
(Rural Texas, p. 39)

Like a Victorian valentine full of hearts and flowers, *Rosewood Casket* spoke to the deepest sentiments of turn of the century Texans. The song bears an early copyright (1870), and was based on a very popular theme during that era—i.e., dying for love.

ROSEWOOD CASKET

In a little rosewood casket
That is resting on my stand
Is a package of love letters
Written by my true love's hand.

Will you go and get them, sister?
Will you read them o'er to me?
For oft time I've tried to read them,
But for tears I could not see.

Read each precious line so slowly,
That you may not miss a one,
For the precious hand that wrote them,
His last word for me is done.

You have got them, now, dear sister,
Come and sit upon my bed,
And press gently to your bosom,
This poor throbbing, aching head.

Tell him that I never blamed him,
Not an unkind word was spoke,
Tell, oh tell him, sister, tell him,
That my heart in coldness broke.

You have finished now, dear sister;
Will you read them o'er again?
While I listen to you read them,
I will lose all sign of pain.

While I listen to you read them,
I will gently fall asleep
To wake again with Jesus,
Darling sister, do not weep.

Place his letters and his locket,
All together o'er my heart,
And the little ring he gave me
Never from my fingers part.

THE GALVESTON STORM
(Urban Texas, pp. 40 and 41)

The Galveston Storm was written about the devastating hurricane that hit the Gulf Coast on September 8, 1900. Some five to seven thousand lives were lost as lashing winds reached 100 miles an hour and parts of Galveston were under five feet of water. When the wind shifted, the city was inundated by a five-foot tidal wave. The Galveston storm was the worst natural disaster ever to hit Texas.

THE GALVESTON STORM

The sun was brightly shining down
In good old Texas state.
All hearts were gay and happy
With no thought of cruel fate.

The children played upon the streets
Without a single care,
While hum of toil and business
Floated on the summer air.

But suddenly the sky grew dark;
Then came the wind and rain,
Until the country round was battling
With the hurricane.

And as the tempest raged and roared
The angry gulf was sped
Along the coast until the host
Was numbered with the dead.

Many a life went out that day
And stilled a heart that was warm
For homes and lives were swept away
In that terrible Texas storm.

In Galveston alone, six thousand
Felt the hand of death,
While twenty towns were withered
By the cyclone's cruel breath.

How many souls were lost that day
No one will ever know,
But thousands weep with hearts bowed down
Beneath the cruel blow.

And all the nation mourns
September 8, the fatal day
That Texas felt the storm that swept
Those homes and lives away.

BEAUTIFUL TEXAS
(The State Capitol, pp. 42 and 43)

Beautiful Texas was written by W. Lee O'Daniel five years before he was elected governor of Texas. During this time he formed a very popular musical group called the Light Crust Doughboys, which was featured on a radio program he directed.

In 1938, completely unknown in politics, O'Daniel entered the Democratic race for governor against twelve opponents. Campaigning on a platform of "Less Johnson grass and politicians, and more smokestacks and businessmen," he stumped the state with another musical group, the Hillbilly Boys, and was elected without a runoff.

BEAUTIFUL TEXAS

You have all read the beautiful stories,
Of the countries far over the sea,
From whence came our ancestors
To establish the land of the free,
There are some folks who still like to travel
To see what they have over there,
But when they go look, it is not like the book,
And they find there is none to compare.

(Chorus)
Beautiful, Beautiful Texas
Where the beautiful bluebonnets grow,
We're proud of our forefathers
Who fought in the Alamo,
You can live on the plains or the mountains,
Or down where the sea breezes blow
And you're still in beautiful Texas,
The most beautiful State that I know.

Indian Paint Brush and Bluebonnets

OVER THERE
(World War I, pp. 44 and 45)

George M. Cohan was already a famous show-business personality when he wrote *Over There*. Born into a vaudevillian family, he grew up on stage; but at age twenty-six became an over-night sensation in "Little Johnny Jones"—a Broadway musical in which he played the lead role and for which he wrote the words and music.

He was at home when he read in the papers that America had declared war on Germany. He later revealed: "I read those war headlines and I got to thinking and humming to myself—and for a minute I thought I was going to dance. I was all finished with the chorus and the verse by the time I got to town, and I also had a title."

In recognition of his authorship of "Over There" and "You're a Grand Old Flag," George M. Cohan was awarded the Congressional Medal of Honor.

OVER THERE

Johnnie get your gun,
   get your gun, get your gun,
Take it on the run,
   on the run, on the run;
Hear them calling you and me;
Every son of liberty.
Hurry right away,
   no delay, go today,
Make your daddy glad
   to have had such a lad,
Tell your sweetheart not to pine,
To be proud her boy's in line.

(Chorus)
Over there, over there,
   send the word, send the word over there,
That the Yanks are coming,
   the Yanks are coming,
The drums rum-tumming ev'ry where.
So prepare, say a pray'r,
   send the word, send the word to beware,
We'll be over, we're coming over,
And we won't come back
   till it's over, over there.

THE DYING TOOLIE
(Oil Boom, pp. 46 and 47)

The Dying Toolie is one of the rare oil boom songs. This scarcity has been said to be partly due to the fact that drilling does not require work needing a constant rhythm—such as chopping cotton, laying rails, or hoisting sails. This song gives us a glimpse into the lives of early Texas oil field workers.

THE DYING TOOLIE

O, the toolie of a drilling crew
With short and feverish breath
In a boarding house in Beaumont
Lay near the point of death.

His driller stood beside him
While his life did ebb away
And bent with pitying glances
To hear what he did say.

The toolie's lips did tremble
As he took the driller's hand
And said, "No more will I temper bits
To pierce the Texas sand;

"No more the boiler I will fire
Nor climb the derrick high;
No more I'll eat a midnight lunch
Beneath the southern sky.

"A message I would have you take
To my pleasant home of yore
For I was born in Franklin
On the Allegheny shore.

"Tell my father not to shed a tear
Nor bow his aged head
When you gently break to him the news
That his eldest son is dead;

"That the precepts of his teachings
I have ever kept in mind
And never skipped a board bill
Though it took my hard-earned dimes.

"Tell my mother that her loving son
When death was drawing nigh,
Looked forward to a brighter home
And did not fear to die;

"That in my dreams I saw her form
Beside the cottage door
In that far-off home in Franklin
On the Allegheny shore."

The toolie's lips were silent
There was one angel more;
Saint Peter wrote "Tim Murphey
From the Allegheny shore."

DEEP IN THE HEART OF TEXAS
(World War II, pp. 48 and 49)

Deep in the Heart of Texas is a 1941 audience participation song. It has been featured in over a dozen films; and was so popular during World War II that even in areas where people were unable to speak or understand English, they could often say, "Deep in the Heart of Texas!"

DEEP IN THE HEART OF TEXAS

There is a land, western land,
Mighty wonderful to see,
It is the land I understand,
And it's there I long to be.

(Chorus)
The stars at night are big and bright,
(clap, clap, clap, clap)
DEEP IN THE HEART OF TEXAS.
The prairie sky is wide and high,
(clap, clap, clap, clap)
DEEP IN THE HEART OF TEXAS.
The sage in bloom is like perfume,
(clap, clap, clap, clap)
DEEP IN THE HEART OF TEXAS,
Reminds me of the one I love,
(clap, clap, clap, clap)
DEEP IN THE HEART OF TEXAS.

The coyotes wail along the trail,
(clap, clap, clap, clap)
DEEP IN THE HEART OF TEXAS.
The rabbits rush around the brush,
(clap, clap, clap, clap)
DEEP IN THE HEART OF TEXAS.
The cowboys cry, "Ki-yip-pee-yi,"
(clap, clap, clap, clap)
DEEP IN THE HEART OF TEXAS.
The dogies bawl, and bawl, and bawl,
(clap, clap, clap, clap)
DEEP IN THE HEART OF TEXAS.

THE STREETS OF LAREDO
(Modern Texas and Space, pp. 50-52)

The Streets of Laredo is one of the greatest and most enduring of the cowboy songs; but it did not originate as part of the cattle culture.

In about 1790 there was an Irish version that identifies the young man as a soldier who calls for the military drums to sound his death march. In an English version, called "The Unfortunate Rake," the young man is found dying at Lock Hospital, "wrapped in flannel, so hard was his fate." Later the setting for the song was St. James Infirmary in London.

The song was carried over the ocean and eventually across America. One of the earliest cowboy versions was set in Dodge City in Tom Sherman's barroom. Here the cowboy is dying of a gunshot wound; but the song retains the words, "I know I've done wrong"—which is a holdover from the soldier's dissolute life.

(Lyrics to *The Streets of Laredo* may be found on p. 52.)